Christine.

MW00513238

With my very
best wishes,

Chris.

CHRIS@VERBALIDENTITY.COM

STRONG LANGUAGE

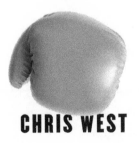

STRONG LANGUAGE

THE FASTEST, SMARTEST, CHEAPEST MARKETING TOOL YOU'RE NOT USING

CHRIS WEST

HOUNDSTOOTH
PRESS

STRONG LANGUAGE

The Fastest, Smartest, Cheapest Marketing Tool You're Not Using

ISBN   978-1-5445-2356-9 *Hardcover*
        978-1-5445-2355-2 *Paperback*
        978-1-5445-2357-6 *Ebook*
        978-1-5445-2354-5 *Audiobook*

To Mum and Dad, for giving me a love of reading.

To Caroline, for showing me the power of determination.

To Charlotte, for giving me so much more love and support than I ever imagined, or come to think of it, deserved.

And to Clemmie and Caspar – every day is a great day when I hear your voices. Love you.

Contents

Acknowledgements

Writing a book is easy. All you have to do is excuse yourself from family commitments for a year or two. So first, I'd like to say there wouldn't be a word on a page here without the continued love, encouragement, and support of Charlotte, and the trust of Caspar and Clemmie. Thank you.

Before I'd ever thought about writing a book, some people inspired me to think about writing. My first Creative Director, Simon Dicketts, was also my first editor: he'd carefully look at a headline I'd written, then put a thumb over a word and say, 'Do we really need that, do we, hmmm?' He was always right. To him, my other Creative Directors, and my Editors, thank you.

I wouldn't have even been in that room (and a few other good places) if it weren't for the encouragement of one of the world's most talented art directors and nicest people, John Messum. Thank you, mate.

My thinking has been inspired so often by one of the world's other most decent, brilliant people, Adam Morgan. He literally wrote the book on Challenger Brands, and he's never stopped giving me advice. I almost wish you'd go and read his book *Eating the Big Fish* instead of reading this one. Almost. Adam, thank you so much.

Other writers I've been lucky enough to meet and be inspired by include Sean Doyle, Tim Riley, and Matt Rudd. Thank you for encouraging me so often, even when you didn't realise you were.

When this book was half an idea, some people were generous with their time and advice. Thank you for everything, Susy Korb, Anthony Finbow, Fred Burt, Cedric Krummes, Liz McGrath, Simon Spilsbury, David Clark, and Giles Spackman. I'm sure I've forgotten someone here, so to you – thank you and my apologies.

When this book was almost a book, everything was made a lot easier by having a great photographer – thank you, Mocho – and a great publishing team: thank you, Rose, Brian, and the team at Scribe.

I am lucky.

Introduction

It could be a fright dream.

You find yourself in a big office, sitting behind a big desk with piles of papers scattered across it. It feels familiar but somehow not. There are 20 people in there, sitting, standing, younger, older, all staring at you. It takes a moment to work out what's hand-painted onto the other side of your office door:

Editor

You look down at the piles of papers on your desk: each of them is an article, and all the people in the room are watching you and waiting for you to approve or improve their story. They need you to edit all those words, no time to waste, the presses are waiting. Fifty thousand words in the voice of this newspaper you've somehow found yourself in charge of.

You flick through the papers – some writing is great; some is just terrible. But why's the great great and the terrible terrible? It'll be all right if you can just work fast enough. Then a feeling of nausea surges through you: this is just today's newspaper.

Tomorrow there'll be another 50,000 words to edit. A bell starts ringing, the red light in the corner of your office starts flashing: the presses are turning, giant rolls of newssheet are now running through them. They're coming out totally blank. The bell keeps ringing. And ringing.

You wake up. The bell is your alarm clock. It's just a dream.

You get into the office with the sound of the alarm still echoing round your head. And there are already 20 people queueing up outside, and each of them has a piece of paper in their hand: the new web copy, the new social media campaign, the new contact centre scripts, the CEO's speech, the Head of Investor Relations' quarterly report, the packaging copy, the internal comms campaign, the new employee's pack. Everyone is looking at you expectantly. And then the phone on your desk starts ringing, clashing with the alarm that's still sounding in your head. It's the CEO's line. Why's she calling? What does she want? Your arm reaches out; why are you wearing pyjamas in front of these people? You pick up the phone, but it doesn't stop ringing.

And now you wake up for real.

And as you lie there, you work it out in your head: every day, you're responsible for more words coming out of your company than the Editor of the Guardian newspaper had to put into today's printed edition. But unlike the Editor of the Guardian, you've never been told how to edit, guide, or inspire writers. And unlike newspapers, no one's choosing to hear what you want to say.

If you want your brand to grow, if you don't want to have to squander budget just to win attention, if you want to engage your customers, if you want to build loyalty, if you want to shine in Customer Experience, if you want to motivate your company, if you want your packaging to tell your story, you have to find a way to say everything your brand wants to say, and say it in a voice that grabs everyone's attention.

In the last ten years, the number of channels has exploded: web, social, CRM, loyalty comms, Customer Service, internal comms, and there's still advertising, packaging, brochures, investor relations, legal, and all the rest.

But these aren't one-way channels. Today, consumers expect to be in a dialogue with brands they like. And who hangs around for a response in a real dialogue? You now have to be able to trust your writers to send out brand comms through multiple channels, at greater volumes than ever before, and without you ever seeing it. Are they staying on-brand? Are they interesting? Are they flexing the writing to suit the channel's environment so you're not showing up like Dad at a school disco?

When budgets are being cut, expectations are rising, and there's less time than ever before to do anything, you have to learn a fast and effective way to define your brand voice and guide all your writers in using it.

But everyone can write, can't they?

The truth is, everyone can't write. Not well. Not in a way that makes your brand stand out. But everyone can be taught how to do it.

Everyone can be taught to write in a strong brand voice. A voice that *does* sound different and engages people, painting pictures in their minds. A voice which can be consistently on-brand but also flexes to suit the moment and the channel. It is possible for you to critique your writers so they stay on track and march out of your office inspired. It's possible to walk through your contact centre and not cringe at how someone's describing your brand. You can be regularly signing off Version 2 instead of Version 22. You can field a call from a member of the Board and describe objectively why your team's written something in a certain way. You can direct your writers to use language to reposition your product into a new category. And you never ever need to look at something your brand's written and say, 'It's not right, it's not us, but I just don't know what's wrong with it.'

This book is how you do all that. It'll show you how your brand language always works on three levels – and how you can make those three levels reinforce each other. It'll show how you can achieve Quick Wins to get the program moving, how you can align all your writers – internal and agency – with that voice, how you manage and inspire your writers, and how you can build the processes (and the budget) for permanent change.

Best of all, you can have a brand voice that establishes your brand as world-class.

We humans are language animals. We invented language to share ideas and deepen relationships. We invented brands for the same reasons. And so, an authentic, differentiated brand voice is uniquely suited to building understanding, building relationships, and building your businesses.

All you have to know is how to build your brand voice.

Here's how you can do it.

SECTION 1

WHAT A WORLD-CLASS BRAND LANGUAGE CAN DO FOR A BUSINESS

Chapter 1

Language moves people

Do you remember how much we all hated supermarkets' self-service checkouts when they were introduced?

As much as anything, that hate was the result of a failure of language.

(And not just the robotic voice which passive-aggressively accused you of putting an 'unexpected item in the bagging area'.)

The self-service checkouts were introduced without the super-markets telling us why. And, in the absence of a narrative, people made one up.

More machines? That'll be the capitalist supermarket owners saving costs by further dehumanising the experience.

But what would you have done to get those checkouts quickly accepted so you could start seeing the savings you'd panned?

Perhaps you'd have done what the supermarkets did: invest even more – this time in arcane behaviour science – and rearrange your floorplan so that all the self-service checkouts are bunched around the exit, subtly suggesting that self-serve will help you get out of the store faster.

That took about three years and millions of pounds.

Or you could've used language to persuade people to like the machines more: you'd have introduced variations in the pitch and cadence of each machine's voice, making it sound more human and avoiding that reverb when five machines all spoke in synch.

That'd only have taken a year and about a tenth as much.

But think what else language could have done for you.

By its nature, language is designed to be quick ('TIGER!'). It's designed to build relationships ('I love you'). And it's designed to convey complicated new ideas ('The quality of mercy is not strained'? Try drawing that!).

And it can also, when someone uses their imagination, be the cheapest marketing tool you have. Because it's language which creates ideas in people's minds, and if you can change the language, you can create new ideas.

Imagine that on the morning the self-serve checkouts were introduced, you'd grabbed a big, fat marker pen, a piece of white card, and some string and hung a sign over the self-checkout lane which said: 'Express Checkout'.

In just two minutes, at the cost of a pen, and with all the infrastructure of a step ladder and two pins, you'd have used language to help people understand exactly what was in it for them if they used a self-service checkout.

And in a way, that's what language does all the time: it explains, it labels, it signposts and helps us navigate the world.

When you understand how a category is subtly kept in check by unspoken rules of what you can and can't say in that category, then you can tilt the category in your favour just by breaking a rule and saying something different. Think what Oatly's done.

When you want to make people think about your brand every day instead of once a week, you can integrate your brand into culture by updating its language. Just be like 'Netflix and chill'.

Or, when your brand's category can no longer give you the growth you want, you can swap categories just by swapping language. Remember when Lucozade was only used for recovering from illness?

When you want to show how your product outperforms expectations, then it's time to make your language outperform. You don't have to talk like Elon Musk, but we can all learn from how he positioned electric cars as fast by calling Tesla's sports mode 'Ludicrous'.

And inside a business, just as much as outside it, language helps us understand what we're doing, what we're trying to create, and the way we're going to go about it.

And to make that happen, you need a simple framework to understand how language works, then get everyone in your team aligned with it.

But first, I want to tell you something about yourself you might not have realised.

> **LANGUAGE IS THE FASTEST, SMARTEST, CHEAPEST MARKETING TOOL**

Chapter 2

Language creates identity

Did you realise you're an expert in linguistics?

That's right. In a subject that only a handful of college students ever study, you're a pro.

It's like you were *born* to do this.

Even more weirdly, you're an expert in forensic linguistics: you have an uncanny ability to gather evidence about someone or something's character just from the words they utter.

How can I be so sure?

It's not just because I've said it to thousands of people before and was right each time.

It's because you *were* born to do it. You are a homo sapiens: you are a language animal.

And as a modern twenty-first-century homo sapiens, you're a commercially attuned, semiotically-primed, language animal.

You're hearing and reading thousands of words a day and instinctively forming an opinion of the identity of the brand, organisation, or person who would utter those kinds of words.

Let me give you an example.

Later in this chapter, you'll see a hundred words written by two different car companies: Mini and Ferrari.

Of course, if you see (or hear) a Ferrari drive past you, you'd probably recognise it as a Ferrari instantly. More than just the badge, there's the dialect of a Ferrari's aerodynamic curves.

And if you saw a Mini going in the opposite direction, you'd be just as quick to pick up its distinctive, differentiated shape and size. Perhaps you'd even subconsciously register its little 'brand winks', like the half Union Jack pattern of its taillights.

We both know there's a wide variety of physical things – shape, noise, colour – that you can control when you're creating the identity of a distinctive, differentiated car.

But language? Is there so much to play with?

The 100 words below are extracts of genuine copy taken from Mini's and Ferrari's websites. Each piece of writing is talking about the same thing: how their car takes a corner.

But I've anonymised the car brands, removing any visual cues: no logo, photography, colours, or layout.

Have a read, then I'll ask you one simple question.

Car Brand X

Born to corner. Driving a [X] is a ton of fun, thanks to
its legendary go-kart handling. We could go on about
its lightning-quick responses and glue-like grip...

Car Brand Y

The [Y] embraces the Side Slip Control 6.0 concept, which
incorporates an algorithm that delivers a precise estimate of
sideslip to the onboard control systems. The SSC 6.0 integrates
systems such as the E-Eff, F1-Trax, SCM-E Frs, and [Y] Dynamic
Enhancer, the latter debuting in the Race Position on the [Y]
Roma. The aim of the 5-position manettino is to make the [Y]
handling and grip even more accessible by extending the setting
ranges thanks to the introduction of the Race position.

So, here's the question: which of these pieces of copy was written
by Ferrari and which was written by Mini?

Easy, right?

Words on their own created an identity in your mind.

How?

Was it the particular words themselves?

Was it some tonal quality that each piece of copy had?

Behind the words and the structure that were present on the
page, was there an emerging sense of the who might say this or
their particular view of how the world should be?

Or was it all three?

The answers to those questions form the framework for every great brand voice.

> **YOU CAN USE LANGUAGE TO CREATE A POWERFUL BRAND IDENTITY**

Chapter 3

Every brand voice works on three levels

How was it that you managed to identify instantly, and with no visual clues, which piece of copy came from Mini and which belonged to Ferrari?

The Mini vs. Ferrari exercise is a good way of introducing the idea of verbal identities in a workshop. Whether you have a roomful of CMOs, interns, Customer Experience directors, packaging designers, writers, or nonwriters, ask them how they could instantly tell which brand was speaking in each piece of copy, and some of the things you'll hear are:

'"Go-kart handling"? No way would Ferrari describe themselves with those words.'

'Yeah', someone else will say, 'Go-karting is all about fun, a Ferrari's much more serious.'

'Exactly, a Ferrari's for serious drivers, a Mini's not. A Ferrari is for people who want highly crafted, technical cars. People that love speed.'

'The second piece of copy seems really aloof, smug, exclusive – "you either know what we're talking about, or you're not really one of our type of people."'

None of the comments shows any specialist car knowledge. All are comments about the language which was used. And the comments about the language can be sorted into three levels.

On the highest level, the brands' language created an overall impression about the worldview of the people who produced the car and the people who drive it: 'A Ferrari is for people who...' or 'Ferrari would never...' This is an Overarching Narrative that guides what the brand will talk about and the angle they take on anything they talk about.

It's about the manufacturer's worldview, not the product they've made.

Mini seems to want a world where you just jump in your car and have fun. The Ferrari marketing team seems much more interested in producing the ultimate sports car.

There's a second set of comments that people make, and at this level, people will often use a lot of adjectives. Like 'sporty', 'self-serious', 'technical', 'tongue-in-cheek'. What they're doing is attributing a personality to the car via the personality of the copy. Instead of revealing some feelings about the manufacturer's view on the world, this is now about the actual product. You might even get a hint of the kind of people who've commissioned the copy – fun lovin' or engineer types.

Finally, when you look back over the comments that people have made, you'll see they were using their forensic linguistics skills to zero in on the Nuts and Bolts of the copy. At this level of the language, they've built up an impression of the identity of the brand from the use (or avoidance) of particular words, especially whether jargon is used or avoided: 'E-Eff, F1-Trax, SCM-E Frs' or 'go-kart'.

But there are other elements of the copy's construction at this level which are equally revealing. The two brands have different average sentence lengths. Ferrari's copy has no sentence shorter than 25 words. Mini has a sentence of three words.

Another element on this level is grammar. Sometimes, that's about writing in the impersonal third person or the warmer first-person plural. Sometimes, it's about formality of grammar and whether you are 'allowed' to write like people speak.

Readers, colleagues, customers, investors, journalists – they all make these kinds of instant, instinctive assessments about a company from the three levels of its language.

And these three levels all have to reinforce each other in order to make sense.

To explain, let's switch on the Verbal Identity drone and take a flight.

> **BRAND LANGUAGE ALWAYS WORKS ON THREE LEVELS**

Chapter 4

Why there are no skyscrapers in downtown Mountain View, California

We're at 10,000 ft. What kind of a place does this look like to you?

Sometimes in a workshop, people hesitate. The most obvious things go unmentioned. Let me prompt you a little, just in case.

Do you think this is an aerial photograph of Stone Age England? Obviously not: we can see modern buildings, a highway, sports pitches.

(And for the slower members of the class, it's worth pointing out that there are very few remaining aerial photographs from the Stone Age.)

What can we see?

There's a mix of industrial spaces, housing, infrastructure of roads and a railway, a park with a lake, and other large areas of green here and there. And it's a city rather than a town because even at this height, it sprawls outside of the photo.

Up here at 10,000 ft, we can see this area's narrative: the story it's telling us is that this is a medium-sized, modern city (American?) for people who want to live in family-sized houses, with easy access to their commutes and somewhere to spend their downtime at weekends.

Let's come down to 1,000 ft. What can we see?

At this level, we get a strong sense of the personality of the neighbourhood. We can see that the tone of the residential area is 'orderly' or 'modest'.

The nonresidential area in the bottom left? That looks to me like a commercial space, maybe a light industrial factory, but definitely not, for example, a China mega mall.

Everything in the personality here at 1,000 ft is consistent with the narrative that was established at 10,000 ft.

Let's come down to Ground Level and see where we land.

There are paved areas where a large number of pedestrians can walk. Big windows, bike racks for 20 bikes.

All of those Ground Level features are consistent with the personality of the neighbourhood which we saw established at 1,000 ft. For example, the building has a glass atrium, but it's not the thrusting extrovert statement you might find in Manhattan. It is relatively modest. But it's not mud hut modest – it's still modern brick and stone.

In fact, all three levels, from 10,000 ft to 1,000 ft to Ground Level, are consistent and reinforce each other.

The building is, in fact, a repurposed mall, now the headquarters of a company called X. It's Alphabet's 'Moonshot Factory' and one of Silicon Valley's most mind-bendingly imaginative companies. It's the place where the Waymo driverless car company was nurtured, where drone delivery of medicines is being pioneered, and where contact lenses which measure your blood glucose levels have been developed.

It also happens to be one of the places where we created a brand voice which works on all three levels: an Overarching Narrative, a personality (or Tone of Voice), and the Ground Level Nuts and Bolts.

In Mountain View, if you submitted a plan to demolish X's building and apply for a 120-floor, 1,800 ft high skyscraper, you'd soon be fighting the town planners. It's just not that kind of area.

Similarly, if you referred to X as an 'R & D lab' in a piece of recruitment copy, then it'd be rejected. X thrives by persuading the world's best minds to come there and create world-changing tech, rather than doing R & D. It's not just the choice of words: it's about X's narrative and personality.

If you're writing Ferrari's copy, you could try and drop the F-bomb, but you'd be fighting Ferrari's CMO: Ferrari's copy's just not that kind of place. You could go into great technical detail of the brakes in Mini's copy, but Mini's copy's not that kind of place.

In successful brand language, just as in a successful company or coherent neighbourhood, all three levels reinforce each other.

> **YOU HAVE TO MAKE SURE THE THREE LEVELS OF YOUR BRAND VOICE REINFORCE EACH OTHER**

Case study #1

How an ambitious tech firm improved their content's
performance and started winning the talent war by
defining their brand voice on all three levels.

How do you recruit the best people? How do you align them with your culture once they arrive? How do you change what the world thinks of you?

These are questions that every leadership team asks itself, but the leadership team at this Silicon Valley company faced an even greater challenge. They were spun off from their global parent company specifically to invent technology which solves massive world problems. Their job is to make a reality of those big ideas which the rest of the world thinks are crazy.

To succeed, incremental change wasn't part of the plan. To solve the world's biggest problems, you need 10× the technology and 10× the thinking.

Their CMO's role was more than marketing or creating a Tone of Voice for a tech firm. It was about shaping internal culture, winning the hearts and minds of world leaders, and competing for the world's best brains against NASA, every university research lab, and every cash-rich venture capital firm in the world.

But the CMO also knew that to produce a 10× change in product development, every stage of your pipeline, from attracting talent to releasing new products into the commercial world, has to outperform everyone else's. And so, your language has to outperform as well.

Unfortunately, there wasn't 10× as much time in her team's week as anyone else's. What can you do?

She decided to codify their company's language so that it perfectly captured their unique ethos. Much more than merely creating a Tone of Voice, the language had to project the company's exceptional culture and ambition.

Through a series of workshops, 1:1 interviews, desk work, and creative development, we helped the leadership team to see the narrow path their language had to steer between world-changing ambition and hubris. It had to keep its research secret yet never seem secretive. It had to persuade people to change their lives and come and work with them, even while projects may yet only be an idea in someone else's head.

When you're truly trying to change the world, you might immediately think about creating a big, ambitious Overarching Brand Narrative. But unless the brand voice lives that out in its personality and its choice of Ground Level Nuts and Bolts, the ambition will seem fake.

The team realised that the Overarching Narrative at 10,000 ft had to be explicit about the world's problems, their scale, and the company's belief that tech would overcome those problems.

At 1,000 ft, this was reinforced by a Tone of Voice which amplified the defining characteristics of the people who worked there, including their curiosity and simplicity, while steering clear of ever dumbing down.

At Ground Level, the team saved themselves hundreds of hours by being clear on the words and phrases they do and don't use and their approach to grammatical rules.

We always say that creating the verbal guidelines is only 49% of the task. The bigger part is encouraging everyone to use the new language.

In Phase II of the project, we worked with some of those bright minds to help them understand how language works on three levels, how those levels reinforce each other, and the daily decisions they could make to reinforce their culture and communications through the right language.

After two months of work with the client team, a new set of guidelines was in place, the key leadership members were inducted, and training was successfully rolled out.

The proof of success is always whether the new language guidelines are lived every day, by everyone. These were.

But a greater test we applied to ourselves was to make sure that we had helped the communications team become 10× more productive in their voice – without any impact on their workload or budget.

We are delighted to say that we passed this test as well.

A refresher

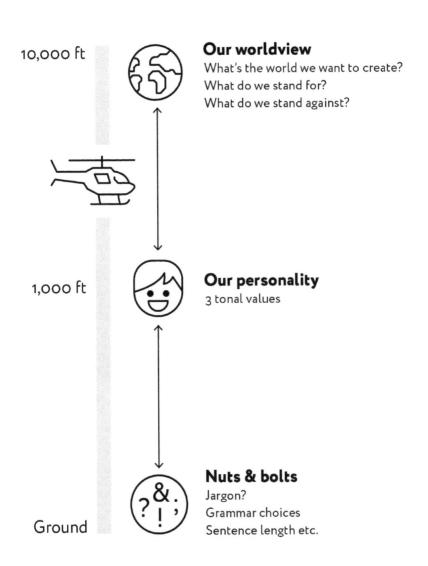

10,000 ft

Our worldview
What's the world we want to create?
What do we stand for?
What do we stand against?

1,000 ft

Our personality
3 tonal values

Ground

Nuts & bolts
Jargon?
Grammar choices
Sentence length etc.

SECTION 2

CREATING A WORLD-CLASS BRAND VOICE

10,000 FT: HOW TO CREATE YOUR BRAND VOICE NARRATIVE

Chapter 5

What exactly is a Brand Voice Narrative?

I remember back in early 2000, being on a long flight and reading a *Wall Street Journal* article about businesses starting to use narrative.

Interesting, I thought. How can a commercially driven organisation use something that goes, 'Once upon a time...'? How can they benefit from saying there's a beginning, middle, and end to everything?

Well, we were all naïve at the start of 2000. Since then, the theory of 'narrative' has been unwrapped and used as a powerful communications tool.

Narratives are simple rules which help us navigate the world.

We see two events in time and automatically consider them related: *this* event was followed by *that* event, and there was some relationship between them *because* they happened so close together in space or time.

And when we're confronted with something new, our brains automatically try to find a fit for it in our library of preexisting storylines, so we can predict what we need to do with it.

So, in a world full of signals and noise and novel events, our brains automatically use narrative thinking to make sense of the world and our relationship with it.

(And our brains are confounded when something doesn't follow the expected narrative. Hence comedy.)

It's a critical ability.

Imagine your ancestor 12,000 years ago, standing in the African grasslands. The grass is up above their head. Two hundred metres away, they hear a low grumbling growl.

A lion?

The next moment, they hear the sounds of a quarter-ton animal rushing through that grass towards them.

Definitely a lion.

If their brain wasn't able to quickly link those first two events and conclude what a likely third event would be, then they wouldn't be your ancestor because you wouldn't be.

This default-to-narrative is at work in people's brains when they hear your brand speaking.

When you have a consistent narrative, your actions don't look random; they look like considered choices. People believe there's an underlying logic at work in your company. Everything you do seems to be driven by a singular view of the world and what you're trying to create in it.

People know what to come to you for and what to expect from their relationship with you.

If the expectations of a narrative aren't met, your audience gets confused, and it's easier for them to walk away rather than add to the burdens of their conscious brain by trying to work out what's going on.

This applies to all of a brand's activities. But because language is such a free-flowing, easily generated medium, defining the narrative of your brand's voice is essential.

When you define for your writers that 10,000 ft narrative of your brand voice, they can be consistent on your worldview and what people should expect of you.

That's one of the things that the Ferrari and Mini copy do so well.

> **DEFINE THE NARRATIVE OF YOUR BRAND'S VOICE, AND YOUR AUDIENCE INSTANTLY ENGAGES WITH YOUR BRAND AND ITS VALUES**

Chapter 6

How Mini and Ferrari use their Brand Voice Narratives

In those 100 words of copy from Ferrari and Mini, you had an instant sense of which brand had written which piece of copy. Part of that was having an idea of the particular view of the brand that had written it.

Each piece of copy had a strong sense of narrative.

Not the 'Once upon a time…' kind, but a sense of 'This is the world we believe in…so we're these kinds of people, with these kinds of values…and we stand against this kind of thing'.

Ferrari believes in a world in which driving your sports car should be a fast, technical, and luxurious experience. Mini believes in a world where driving your car should be fun.

They are the two different worlds that the two different brands are trying to create.

But it's also critical when you're defining the narrative to define the 'kind of people' behind a brand.

Here's why.

While Mini believes in a world where driving your car should be fun, they could inhabit that world in a number of different ways. For example, they could build cars which are shaped like cats and have engines that purr. That would make driving your car fun, too. But they're not that kind of people. They're the kind of people who love go-kart handling.

The makers of Ferrari could choose to inhabit the world of sports cars in the same way that the team behind the Atom car brand do: stripping off the roof and not bothering with passenger seats, carpets, radio, body panels, or just about anything else. Instead, Ferrari creates a fast, technical, and luxurious sports car experience by being the kind of people who decide to put both the most advanced automotive mechanical technology into their car, along with things like carpets and a passenger seat so you can share the experience with someone.

So, defining what kind of people you are in your narrative helps explain how you're going about creating the world you believe in.

Strategy is about choice. And being as clear about what you stand against as what you stand for helps you be clear about what fights you're going to pick when you're communicating.

For Mini, one of the things they stand against seems to be making the car's engineering something that the reader or driver has to be aware of: it'll get in the way of having fun.

And for Ferrari, one of the things they stand against seems to be trivialising their excellent engineering.

When you answer these three questions: 'What's the world we believe in?', 'So, what kind of people are we?', and 'What do we stand against?', you've created a strong narrative which defines your territory and makes your brand communications coherent.

You'll also have helped all your writers write from a single territory.

By following this narrative, they'll create a differentiated brand which occupies a coherent – and defendable – space in your customers' minds.

Brand teams and customer experience teams are often reluctant to define what they stand against. It seems unnecessarily antagonistic.

But being clear about what you stand against is one of the most powerful elements of your Brand Voice Narrative, whatever position your brand is in. As a nun taught me once.

> **YOUR NARRATIVE IS THE BIG STORY**
> **YOUR BRAND IS ALWAYS TELLING**

Chapter 7

The nun's manoeuvre

I overheard a nun speaking to a neighbour of ours, back when we used to live in Notting Hill. And what the film *Notting Hill* failed to mention was that despite the heterogeneous mix of white Hollywood stars and middle-class, white bookshop staff, the area is intensively conservative in its attitudes to building development.

The nun was distinctly unhappy about the objections the locals had raised to their proposed building works, and I caught just one sentence of her conversation:

'If you're not on our side about this, you're working for the Devil', she told the poor man.

Communication becomes a lot easier when you know what you stand against.

Sure, define what you stand for. (Provided it's not Apple Pie and Mom. Because, well, doesn't everyone stand for that?)

But to make your brand voice really stand out in this world, be prepared to call out what you stand against.

Not just to attract the people who already know that they stand against that, as well.

When you define clearly what you stand against, your brand voice slips an oyster knife into the closed communal mindset, and it gently (or in the nun's case, not so gently) starts teasing people apart.

It opens a gap between people who are also against what you're against and the rest of the world.

And the more of a gap between them that you create, the more definitely divided they become and the more loyal to your brand.

Certainly, you'll have people who feel more definitely opposed to you, but if they're ever vocal about it, claiming how right they are in their choice, they're supporting the basis of your division, reflecting back to those who support you how right they are in *their* choice and reinforcing their loyalty to you.

It's like a small crack appearing in the ice shelf you're standing on. You don't mind which side of the crack you're on when it's small and insignificant. Pick one side, doesn't matter, you're not far from being on the other side when you need to. Or maybe you'll have a leg on either side.

But as the crack becomes more significant, the gap in the middle becomes deeper, and there's suddenly a binary decision to be made: this side or the other side? And certainly, no one wants to fall into the chasm of nothingness in the middle. So, everyone leaps to take a side.

Does all this sound familiar? It was the nun's manoeuvre, and it's been the politicians' strategy recently, both the left and right wings, as populist parties, highly oppositional in nature, have taken power.

In a world of look-alike, sound-alike politicians, and look-alike, sound-alike products, if you don't want to outspend your competitors, you have to hope for a divine miracle to intervene and save you – which the nuns, even with their inside info, weren't prepared to do – or you have to be brutally clear on what you stand for and what you stand against.

> **BEING CLEAR ON WHAT YOU STAND AGAINST IS AS IMPORTANT AS BEING CLEAR ON WHAT YOU STAND FOR**

Chapter 8

Tesla and Google's Brand Voice Narratives

A press release from Tesla states that the company is for 'accelerating the world's transition to sustainable energy'.

What do they stand against? You'll often hear them explicitly state that they're against reliance on fossil fuels.

What kind of people are they? Their Mission Statement opens by stating that the Founders were 'engineers', and as it talks about what they've done, there's an emphasis on creation and manufacture.

With those elements of the voice's narrative defined, it's easy for Tesla's writers to know what to write about and what angle to take on it.

Google (the search engine company, not its parent, Alphabet) has a Mission Statement which says it believes in a world where the world's information is organised, universally accessible, and useful.

Google talks about how they're the kind of people who are 'dedicated to improving people's lives'.

And what are they against? I think behind their communications is the sense that they're against a lack of order – and possibly that's why sometimes they have problems with the messy humanness of humans.

If I were a Google writer or a Tesla writer, and it was half-past eight on a Thursday night, with copy needed on your desk tomorrow morning, I'm pretty sure I'd be writing about the right kinds of things.

I've reverse-engineered the Voice Narratives for Tesla and Google.

However, there's one car brand whose Voice Narrative we can be sure about because we helped the brand's leaders create it.

Vauxhall is a mainstream UK car brand, and when we worked with them, they were owned by the same megacorp that owned the German car brand Opel. In fact, many Vauxhalls were effectively rebadged Opels. Now, Opel isn't BMW or Mercedes. But it is a well-built German car with lots of German technological features.

As we worked through our process and talked to the brand teams, some things became clear. The brand and the team behind it believed driving should be fun, not a drag. They were 'egalitarian': valuing a positive, inclusive world. And importantly, they stood against a world where technology is reserved for a few expensive cars.

This is the Brand Voice Narrative we created with them and their agencies:

> We're a forward-looking bunch,
> so let's create a Britain where millions can enjoy driving.
> Let's give people today the quality and technology
> that was once reserved for only a few.
> Let's be optimistic. Let's be energetic.
> Let's do more than just get people from A to B:
> let's make sure they get in and out of their car with a smile.
> What are we waiting for? Let's go!

When everyone read this narrative, something immediately changed: people said that the brand had finally released its potential. Others said that it helped bring to the surface some qualities that they'd felt were in the brand but had never been able to fully explain. And some people just said, 'That's going to make writing copy a whole lot easier.'

A Brand Voice Narrative is a powerful asset. Its power depends on finding something which is authentic, relevant, and differentiating in the brand.

It's hard finding those answers. And reaching agreement on those answers is essential. But when you define what you believe in, the kind of people you are, and the things you stand against, then you have defined your brand voice's narrative. You just need a way of doing that easily.

DEFINE THE WORLD YOU BELIEVE IN, WHAT YOU'RE DOING TO CREATE IT, AND WHAT YOU STAND AGAINST

Chapter 9

Define your Brand Voice Narrative
Part 1: 'Data in'

We've found that the best way to discover a brand voice's narrative is to ask people.

You ask the most senior person you can.

You ask the most junior person you can.

You ask the person who's been at the company the longest.

You ask the person who joined last week and is suffering from the culture shock of what the company is on the inside compared to what they thought it'd be before they arrived.

You ask the person who's been writing those Customer Service letters for 20 years.

You ask the legal department.

You ask Investor Relations.

If they're still alive and sane, you ask the Founder.

In fact, ask as many people as you can, and don't forget to ask external partners, journalists, and analysts who cover the sector.

But, of course, you can't just come right out and ask them what kind of company you're sitting in.

You need to frame the discussion in advance, making sure that people know it's valuable work.

The questions should be carefully prepared to help people give honest answers that are also insightful.

Here are the worksheets we use:

DISCOVERY OF THE BRAND VOICE NARRATIVE.

TO PREPARE IN ADVANCE:

1. Send a personalised email asking for 45 minutes in their diary.

   SJ: Your contribution to the development of the brand voice

   Content:

   Dear xxxx,

   As you might know, [CEO] has asked us to comprehensively define our brand voice so we can engage our audiences.

   I'd appreciate it if you could find 45 minutes for a chat, preferably next week. Please would you let me know what time you have by selecting a slot on the attached Google doc.

   Many thanks,

   xxxxx

2. Prep your questions.

QUESTIONS:

a. Smile when they walk in.
b. Explain: this is just a chat...I'm interested in your personal views... none of this is reported back, so feel free to share anonymously...it's really your personal thoughts that count...I have some questions, they normally take about 30–45 minutes, but they're a guide only....often the most valuable discussions happen when we go off at a tangent...

we're gathering as much information from different people...then we'll use it to build a comprehensive brand voice...

c. Check: is that OK?
d. Questions:

1. Can I just check I understand your role here...?
2. When did you join [this company]?
- [We like to start with a simple question, one that doesn't take a lot of thinking and is personal. It gets the interviewee warmed up.]
3. Thinking back to before you joined, why did you come to [this brand]?
- [This helps the interviewee talk personally about what they saw in the company that made it worth joining. Often the external face of a company is a good clue to the company's worldview.]
4. Can you remember your first week or so here, what surprised you about [this company]?
- [First impressions really do reveal a lot. It's important to ask them to think back, because after a while of working somewhere, what seemed unique or different begins to seem normal.]
5. What do you like most about working here?
6. What do you like least about working here?
7. Is there a place you can point me to, where the Voice is really clear and good?
- [You never know! Maybe the answer's there already. What's important though, is that the most common answer to this question is, 'No, not really'. The advantage of asking the question is that it helps remind everyone you talk to of the purpose of this work.]
8. Imagine that Tesla announced they were now going to use their electric tech to power factories...that seems like a very Tesla thing to do. But imagine instead, they said that powering cars with electricity was just too difficult and expensive to develop, so from now on, they'd be making petrol-powered cars...that would seem very un-Tesla. What – if this company stopped doing it – would seem to take the essence of the company away?

9. What's the biggest challenge of your role?
10.If you had a magic wand, what one thing would make doing your job easier?

e. Thank them.

Remember:

The most critical thing is that whatever definition of Brand Voice Narrative you're building, you also build universal agreement with it. For this reason, at the end of the session, we explain how all the answers will be used and what will happen next.

A tip:

We've found that asking a full set of questions takes about 45 minutes. And it takes about 15 minutes to clear your head and stretch your legs between each interview.

Always take time to explain why you're doing this and your process. This will help you build alignment later on.

And once you have everyone's answers, you just need to know what to do with them.

> **THE BEST WAY TO DEFINE YOUR BRAND VOICE NARRATIVE IS FROM THE INSIDE OUT**

Chapter 10

Define your Brand Voice Narrative
Part 2: 'Information Out'

There are some people who can look at a spreadsheet and see themes emerging immediately. And there are some people who understand language like those people understand numbers: when they look at the results of interviewing ten or a hundred people, they also see themes emerging.

But for anyone who wants to bring their audience along with them as they define a Brand Voice Narrative, a reliable process saves time and money.

Here's how we do it.

Gather together the surveys and – in some lengthy legwork – summarise each person's answer to each question on an index card.

Spread those index cards out on the biggest table you can find.

Then start moving them around.

When you do that, see if you can find one or two answers which seem thematically similar. Then look for some more like that. Then see if there are any other answers which naturally coalesce.

Keep going.

You'll find that after about two hours, you have four or five different groups.

Some answers and index cards will sit lonely on the table. Throw them away. Really. Everyone's view is personal. No one's personal view is wrong. It's just that some views just aren't shared with anyone else. So, throw them away. Discreetly, of course.

Some of the groups will be strong on what your brand believes in; some will be strong on how you see the world. And a few will tell you what you stand against.

The combination of those groups tells some kind of story: they build some kind of worldview.

If it doesn't seem obvious yet, don't worry. Leave it overnight. The trick is to see the picture emerging rather than forcing your own opinions onto the research.

When we worked with Tourneau, the premium multi-brand watch retailer in the States, the owners hadn't invested in it for a long time, and the brand experience was tired. But when we spent time asking people about their company, we found something authentic, relevant, and differentiating that had been overlooked for a long time: each individual's passion for the whole world of watches made them great guides.

Their worldview was that they believed watch enthusiasts should be able to get together in person not just to sell and buy watches but to discuss and compare and dive deep into discovering the whole world of watches. This became the heart of the narrative. And this shaped all of the brand's developments, influencing not just Tourneau's language but a wide range of other elements.

The Brand Voice Narrative inspired the flow of the new website design. Sales teams were hired and trained to be more empathetic. The architects of the new flagship store were inspired to include space for customers and staff to sit together without any visual barriers which implied a sense of 'us and them'.

Sometimes though, when you're asking questions, you'll find that people give answers which are too polite. In that case, you need a special technique to unlock differentiating, uncommon answers.

But I warn you now. It involves swearing. And it works best when the swearing uses the F-bomb.

If you're easily offended, skip the next chapter.

> **YOUR COMPANY'S HIVE MIND
> ALREADY KNOWS THE NARRATIVE
> FOR YOUR BRAND VOICE. ALL
> YOU HAVE TO DO IS LISTEN**

Chapter 11

F**k polite

Sometimes, people are just too polite. When it comes to defining their company or their company's worldview, they say 'the right thing'. And what bloody good is that?

(I warned you there'd be swearing.)

With them, we use 'The Friday Night Pub Test'.

I'd like to do the test on you. Ready?

Imagine I'm asking you about the company you're working for at the moment.

I've let you know that I'm after your own views, your own feelings. There are no wrong answers. It's the personal views which are always the most interesting.

I've assured you that anything you say will be treated confidentially. Nothing you say will be attributed to you.

And we've had a quick chat about how important it is to define the voice of your brand, how it's about more than just the voice; it'll add value throughout your company, help shape beliefs, reduce workload.

You get it. Great.

Then I ask you about how long you've been here. And then I ask you about why you joined.

Oh dear, you said that this seemed like a 'nice' company, 'good people', 'close to the bus stop'. Or maybe you've described it like every company in your sector.

And, apparently, when you joined, there was 'nothing much' different that surprised you about working here.

OK.

So, if it'd be all right, I have another question I'd like to ask you. Is that OK?

Oh good, but listen, I'm sorry. It does involve swearing. Are you OK with that?

Are you sure? Because it is, you know, F-bomb swearing?

OK?

OK.

Great. Well, I was wondering…imagine that it's Friday, and it's been not exactly a tough week but basically a full-on week, and to ease yourself into the weekend, you stop off at your favourite pub or bar for a drink to shake off the week. Do you have a favourite pub or bar?

Oh, sounds great. I don't drink, really. What would you be ordering, Friday at 6 p.m., at the end of a hard week?

A crème de menthe? Interesting.

Well, imagine in your haste to 'lift your elbow' to take a sip and wave goodbye to the week, you knock over the pint of lager belonging to the builder standing next to you.

Oops. He's not happy at all. Big oops.

Time to make amends, and so you offer to buy him another pint. Which he accepts and then feels a little guilty for the hard stares he gave you. He decides to make nice and says, 'So, what do you do?'

What do you answer?

'I'm the CMO of MegaCorp.'

And he says, forever the straightforward builder:

'I've never heard of MegaCorp. What's so fucking good about them, then?'

What do you say?

Not 'we deliver excellence in blah de blah'. Builder man not interested.

What do you say? Straight and to the point?

Whatever you answer now is probably what's best about your company, and it's probably what your company's worldview is.

It's a neat way to get to the narrative that's driving your brand and your brand voice.

Time to gulp your crème de menthe and leave.

Thank you.

Because once you've discovered and codified your narrative, it's time to get back to work and define the tonal values, the personality, of your brand's voice.

> **YOU HAVE TO BREAK THROUGH**
> **POLITENESS TO GET TO THE TRUTH**

Case study #2

How a new Brand Voice Narrative helped
relaunch a British icon: Hunter Boot.

There are few brands which could be proudly worn on the same day by both Prince Charles and Kate Moss, with each of them thinking they were wearing absolutely the best thing for them.

That was the unusual appeal of the green welly made by Hunter. Yet the brand had been in and out of insolvency, unable to make a sustainable profit even while it tried moving production offshore, changing the price points, trying new designs, and a hundred different things recommended to them by management consultants and investors.

In 2012, a new group of investors bought the brand. Like all good investors, they were ambitious and impatient. They brought in a new CEO, who brought in a new Creative Director, and together they asked Verbal Identity to work with them.

Their challenge was simple: if we could identify and distil that magical essence of the green welly which made it so appealing to princes, supermodels, and civilians like you and me, then they could build a full lifestyle brand with a full range, proper distribution, and profile.

And they'd be able to communicate it. So, what kind of a world did Hunter believe in?

What kind of people were behind the brand?

What did they stand against?

With heritage brands, archaeology is critical, and when we heard about the brand's early days, we saw that there was something significant in their origin story.

Hunter Boot was founded in a time of Victorian invention and, in particular, rubberization. This allowed farmers (and hunters) to start relying on their boots in harsher conditions than before.

The wealth that flowed from industrialisation also meant that there was more money for people to travel beyond the domestic fields and explore foreign countries.

Venturing out into the world was clearly something which Hunter believed in. There are some British brands you feel faintly ridiculous wearing when you're abroad. A Barbour in NYC makes you look a bit too spiffy. But there are some brands that seem to capture your pioneering spirit – even if you're only tramping down a rainy Manhattan block.

What was less well-known was that Hunter had continued to innovate and produce high-functioning, ultra-reliable clothing for specialists such as firefighters, who'd come to rely on the brand.

Once we'd understood Hunter's worldview, we needed to understand the kind of people who were behind the brand. So, we put the brand archaeology to one side and conducted a round of carefully constructed interviews with members of the company and its stakeholders. As always, we asked a mix of the long-established and the newly arrived, the designers and the operators, the investors and the employees.

What emerged was a picture of the brand, its people, and some of the things they didn't believe in.

Hunter isn't a brash brand: subtlety is always part of its appeal. Hunter's people clearly believed in the importance of function and reliability more than eye-catching fripperies or exclusivity.

Hunter was a heritage brand, but it believed in progressive heritage, unlike some 'houses' where change is restricted in order to magnify the appeal of a long history.

As we'd defined the kind of world that Hunter believed in, what it stood for and against, and the kind of people who were behind the brand, we'd managed to capture an authentic, relevant, and differentiated narrative for the brand voice. From this, any writer working on the brand would be able to choose accurately what to write about and what angle to take on it.

As soon as the brand positioning was approved by the investors, the company moved up a gear. The advantage of expressing your brand positioning in simple language, rather than complicated semiotics or narrow design cues, is that it can be understood by people throughout the company. It doesn't need interpretation.

So, the magical 13 words and phrases which defined the brand were used by all the departments as the company accelerated. It was as useful to the product designers as to the HR team and the ops team. It gave a rationale for the Finance Team to understand why certain new investments were critical. It informed where stores should open and where they shouldn't. In all of this, it was useful in deciding what was on-brand and what wasn't.

In a very short period of time, a full range of products – with a consistent and coherent unifying story – was produced and showcased at London Fashion Week.

The range was launched through a number of carefully curated brand stores in many different countries around the world.

The essence of the brand had been distilled and bottled, used to build a true brand.

In the first four years, the brand had double-digit growth and returned to profit.

And about five years after our work, I bumped into one of the senior members of the brand team. He told me that those magical 13 words were still used on a daily basis, quoted in formal meetings and corridor conversations, to decide whether a product, an initiative, or a person was on-brand for Hunter.

The greatest value of a brand language is that it builds an identity and gives direction to everyone inside the company as much as it does for the brand's consumers. When we'd defined Hunter's narrative, we realised we'd also written something which could be described as a Mission Statement but was actually much more of a 'Brand Rant'. It captured the history and the positioning of the brand, but it also championed the emotional feelings that the brand had to bring to life to succeed.

What had originally been intended as a written document became such a powerful rant that the Creative Director invested in it and turned it into a short film.

You can still see it here: https://www.youtube.com/watch?v=wj5GZL9df04

1,000 FT: DEFINING YOUR BRAND'S TONE OF VOICE

Chapter 12

What exactly is – and isn't – a brand's Tone of Voice?

If you remember your poor writer, left alone in the building, late at night, copy to be written for tomorrow morning, hearing the heating system creak and wondering whether there's someone there and their mind starting to wonder whether they could pull off a *Die Hard* if there *is* someone there…this poor writer needs to be brought back on track. A clearly defined narrative will help them.

They'll also need to be able to quickly leave their own personality to one side when they're writing and instead adopt the personality of John McClane. Sorry, the personality of your brand.

Personality is important in brand writing. As we are language animals, whenever we hear or read language, we expect it to come from another social animal. When the writing lacks personality, when it's bland, we assume the organisation that created it is bland. But more than that, with bland writing, it's harder for a reader to find any kind of point to latch on to.

Your brand's Tone of Voice is the personality of the brand come to life in language. Just as your packaging or your logo or your sound design have personality, so must your brand voice.

The challenge for writers – and for people who are commissioning them – is that almost all of our writing education has been about taking personality out.

Think of the writing you were taught in science class. It's designed for precision and conformity. Its specific intent (which, by the way, is a pretence) is that there is no authorial overlay: it's written in a way that suggests there was no one choosing a particular word to subtly emphasise a point or that there was no hand choosing which results to keep for presentation (and which to throw away) to make the story seem stronger. When we're taught in science class to write this way, we're being taught to write precisely but impersonally.

If you're a trainee lawyer, you'll find yourself being taught to write in lawyerese: the use of long, complex sentences with multiple subclauses and those subclauses sometimes, though not always, and certainly not by implication being a matter of regulation, having their own subclauses and themselves being present often not without double negatives and words which seem innocent but impede the brain's ability to process the meaning of the sentence, notwithstanding that those very same words are clearly English, such as notwithstanding.

It's like a club. Only if you speak like us can you be us. It's not a matter of education. It's make-work and obfuscation. It should be illegal.

Even in our English lessons, we're often taught to analyse writing in such a way that we dissect it and lay out its parts. Then we're surprised that those parts seem insignificant and lifeless.

The purpose of giving your brand a Tone of Voice isn't to talk like a mindless engineer (unless your brand and business are about being mindless engineers). But neither is it to create a set of flowery prose.

What we're trying to create is the simplest, most effective expression of your brand's personality. And to be effective, your brand's personality, expressed as its Tone of Voice, has to descend naturally from the narrative of your brand's voice.

> ## CREATING A PERSONALITY FOR YOUR BRAND'S VOICE MEANS PEOPLE CAN RELATE TO YOUR BRAND

Chapter 13

How Mini and Ferrari use Tone of Voice

Remember how you instantly decided which was Ferrari's copy and which was Mini's, back in Chapter 2? One of the things you were responding to was the tonal qualities of each brand's voice.

'Playful' is one adjective that people frequently use in workshops to describe Mini's tone. Another tonal value often suggested is 'extrovert'. 'Nippy' and 'energetic' come up a lot as well. All of these adjectives neatly capture the personality of the copy and, so, indicate the personality of the brand.

'British' is also a common suggestion. This is troublesome because there are many types of Britishness – as a Welshman, a Northern Irishman, and a Scotsman will often remind an Englishman. (In Chapter 15, we talk about how you can make the defining words for your tonal values more differentiating.)

I've never seen Mini's brand guidelines, but I can imagine that another tonal value for their copy might be 'imagination': there's something in the origins of the radical design of the original

Mini by Sir Alec Issigonis which still echoes in the legend of the brand.

In Mini's other media (at least in the UK), these tonal values remain strong.

In their brochures, the writers find space for a playful tone:

> Same handling – more handles. It's the icon you love with double the doors.

And even when promoting visits to Mini's factory, the brand's writers bring in the same tonal values:

> This is where the magic happens.

In workshops, when people describe Ferrari's copy, the adjectives people use to describe the tonal values are often more severe, such as 'exclusive' or 'technical'. But these may be reflecting the reader's feelings as they react to the engineering focus of the copy.

Other words include 'excellence' and 'performance'.

The brand team manages to maintain the distinctive brand voice in different media.

On Ferrari's Twitter account, the writers continue with the 'excellence' and 'technical' focus and talk about 'instantaneous power' and 'titanium rods'.

The brochure for the F8 Spider says:

The F8 Spider's greatest achievement is the fact that it unleashes its power instantaneously with zero turbo lag.

The copy is designed to suggest a highly technical engineer wrote it. And it does just that.

In each piece of copy, the personality of the copy is highly successful at creating a sense of the personality of the brand itself.

> **MINI'S TONE OF VOICE ISN'T BETTER OR WORSE THAN FERRARI'S. DIFFERENT VOICES CREATE DIFFERENT IDENTITIES**

Chapter 14

Why you need only three tonal values to define your brand voice's personality

You might have a friend who is funny, lively, smart, and good at looking after people. They don't have to tell you, 'I'm funny, lively, smart and look at me looking after people.' In fact, if they did, they wouldn't be all that funny, lively, and good with people. Instead, those qualities have to shine through in *how* they talk.

It's the same with your brand voice. It should be *how* it talks that creates a personality for your brand.

The simplest way to define the style or personality of your brand's writing is to use a small collection of adjectives and unpack each adjective with a short explanation.

Choosing how many tones or adjectives is almost as important as which ones you settle on.

Two adjectives seem too few. It doesn't give the voice enough room to flex in different situations.

(And who can avoid the temptation, when restricted to just two words, to make them dynamically opposite? Like 'patiently impatient'. As a writer, when I read descriptions like that, instead of being helped to understand the tone or feel excited about the brand, I just slump into conscious unconsciousness.)

Anything more than four tonal values makes it seem like you've been to a jumble sale of adjectives and picked up some on the cheap.

Undoubtedly, you have to appease some forceful voices in the team, but adding more adjectives gives your writers too much room to manoeuvre, and the voice evolves into a mishmash.

Three adjectives seems like a magic number: few enough to keep the Tone of Voice consistent, but still enough to give your writers different values to play with at different times.

There's another piece of logic behind choosing three adjectives as well: too much choice makes choosing harder. When you ask people to choose just three adjectives, there's some rigour and discussion.

(Often, the three values come out of that discussion. In case it doesn't, there's a method you can use in the next chapter).

One good practice in a workshop is to ask people how they'd define your brand's personality by how it thinks, how it feels, and how it does things.

There's another technique you can use to fire up discussion about your brand's tonal values, and it has a 2,000-year track record. Aristotle categorized successful arguments in rhetoric into logos, pathos, and ethos.

For Aristotle, logos was our power to persuade by logic and reason. This is where we are consciously reasoning with the facts of the world. Is our brand big? Fastest? Does our brand take a step-by-step approach in the way it talks? How does our brand use facts to talk about its expertise – lightly (like Mini) or like an engineer (Ferrari)?

Pathos in rhetoric is all about how we use emotions. What kind of tonal values show how our brand 'feels'? Admiration for the world around us, even adoration? With hints of empathy, impatience, or joy?

Finally, there's 'ethos' or the speaker's trustworthiness. Do we, like many new skincare brands and professional services companies, leverage our learning and talk like a 'doctor brand'? Do we show our trustworthiness through 'consideration', always talking about both sides of an argument?

Finally, check the tonal values against the Brand Voice Narrative to make sure they're logically consistent.

As with any creative process, be prepared to throw out the values that every brand team grasps for the first time around. But how do you spot what's an obvious choice? And what can you do when you spot it?

> **YOU NEED ONLY THREE TONAL VALUES TO DEFINE YOUR BRAND VOICE'S PERSONALITY**

Chapter 15

Don't serve apple pie

Unfortunately, sometimes people reach for 'Apple Pie and Mom' values: those things which are *of course* true. But being so universally true, they hold no specific value for your brand.

The most popular adjectives seem to be: 'human', 'friendly', 'warm', and 'approachable'. 'Authentic' is making a fast run up the outside at the moment.

A good test for the obviousness of your adjectives (and hence, whether they'll be nonspecific and empty of value) is to look for the obvious unsuitability of their diametric opposites. Would any brand today want to describe itself as 'inhuman'? Or 'unfriendly', 'cold', and 'distant'? Or even 'inauthentic'?

Instead, to discover the three or four adjectives which can uniquely describe your brand's Tone of Voice, take another look at the table of index cards you created earlier when you were defining the narrative of your brand voice.

Certain answers that you found will seem to naturally fit into their own little subsets.

Perhaps some answers will all fall into a subset which is about the brand's outspokenness. Or maybe some of what came to the surface in the narrative exercise will reflect your brand's energy levels. Or the way your brand gives advice.

Pick up a fresh index card, lay it on top of a subset and see if you can write down a single word to sum up the group underneath it. Which word describes what the cards underneath are all saying or all adding up to?

Then try another word on that index card...does it give a slightly different slant to the group of cards beneath it? Does it feel like that could be true for the personality of your brand voice?

Keep going several times for each group of words.

You might have more than four groups. In which case, you need to see which two groups can be merged and what higher-level adjective can be used to group them together. (For example, do the 'energy' and the 'outspokenness' adjectives both fit under some other, higher concept about your brand striving to be 'heroic'?)

You'll probably end up with a few more than four alternatives – that's OK. Set your intention that you won't use more than four in the end. Have confidence that some things will be sacrificed along the way, while some things will come back in as minor notes supporting another adjective.

Remember to leave it overnight. If you're running workshops, try and stagger them over two days (with a good evening meal for everyone in between). You want the creative side of your brain to work without the bullying rational part. You'll be surprised how many times the fresh light of day can give you the confidence to throw out some of your alternatives.

The test you need to apply finally is:

- Do these adjectives feel true to us?
- Do they feel like our personality, rather than the personality of our sector or industry?

And don't worry if one or two of the words could apply to your competitors. All comedians are funny. But they each have a unique mixture of values that make them unique.

When you have three or four adjectives on a page, you need to define them and 'unpack them' for your writers.

> YOU DON'T NEED TO MAKE EACH OF
> YOUR THREE VALUES UNIQUE.
> BUT THE COMBINATION
> OF THEM MUST BE

Chapter 16

Words aren't numbers

When I say 'six', you're pretty sure I mean the number between five and seven. But when I say 'British', you and I might have totally different ideas in our heads. When you define your Tone of Voice, you need to unpack each of your adjectives so your writers understand what you meant with each particular word.

One of our earliest clients was Fred Perry, the maker of iconic tennis shirts and leisurewear. When we took them through the exercise in Chapter 10, we ended up with three adjectives that defined their brand's Tone of Voice: 'challenging', 'classic', and 'physical'.

But one writer's interpretation of what those words meant would have been different from what someone else writing for the brand might think they mean.

'Classic' could mean 'unchanging' to the CEO but 'out of date' to a brand writer. Someone else might interpret it as 'timeless' and start writing prose inspired by Jane Austen.

The best way to define the Tone of Voice's values is to spend another 25–50 words unpacking exactly what each adjective means.

When we did this with 'Classic', we referenced the brand's unchanging, iconic style. We noted how the voice was never trying to be achingly modern or tricksy. Instead, the copy had a sense of confidence, control, and steadiness that was borne out of its long experience and knowledge of the world. It wouldn't respond to every twist and turn of fashion.

With Mini, if one of their Tone of Voice values is 'playful', it could be interpreted by different writers as entertaining, exciting, or amusing. In fact, the truer sense of the word for Mini's brand voice is, I believe, something to do with how informality lets you be more spontaneous and enjoy yourself more.

It's in these 25–50 words of definition that you'll find a home for the alternative adjectives which you developed earlier but then discarded. They can throw light on the particular slant of meaning that made the final adjective seem right.

Sometimes, of course, we all need a bit of inspiration. If you can find a physical copy of *The Oxford Dictionary of English Etymology*, this will help you. It has a good explanation of the origins of a particular word and how its usage has developed over time. This will help you unpack subtle shades of meaning, allowing you to be clear on what you wanted the adjective to imply and what you wanted it to avoid.

(Why a physical copy? There's something too quick about online dictionaries. Modern search displays only the first 15 or so words, and it means we're all too easily tempted to not look further into a word's subtle nuances and dig into what we really meant.)

A physical dictionary also allows you to take a random walk through words, finding something else that might be just the most apposite adjective.

Sometimes you're not creating a brand voice definition from scratch. And people don't always have the confidence to generate adjectives that separate you from the rest of the pack in your sector.

What then?

Ah, there's an exercise for that, too.

> **CAREFULLY UNPACK EACH OF YOUR THREE VALUES WITH ANOTHER 25–50 WORDS**

Chapter 17

The '5 Hows' technique

I wish it were sunnier today.

I wish I had more hair.

I wish I was a little bit taller. I wish I was a baller.

But sometimes, wishing can't change anything.

And sometimes, you wish you could change the tonal values for your brand's voice that someone settled on before you joined the team. Especially if those values are the dreaded 'human', 'friendly', 'warm', and 'approachable'.

But what if you can't? What then?

Time for some judo. If people are rooted in having generic values, then embracing those values and going into them in more detail will be more successful than outright attack.

You can do it with a reworked version of the '5 Whys' technique, which is used by management consultants to identify the root cause of a problem.

Here's how the original process works.

When something goes wrong, people are always ready to provide a superficial reason for it. To get past that and nearer to the root of the issue, you ask, 'Why?' And by repeatedly asking 'Why?' at each level, you get closer and closer to the real reason.

For example, one of your team misses a group meeting. Here's how the conversation might go:

> Why did you miss the team meeting today?
> *Because my alarm didn't go off.*
>
> Why didn't your alarm go off?
> *Sometimes I forget to set it.*
>
> Why do you sometimes forget to set it?
> *I don't, erm, it's well, erm, because I don't like the team meetings.*
>
> Why don't you like the team meetings?
> *Because I can't stand your constant questioning.*
>
> Really? Why can't you stand my constant questioning?
> *Because I usually haven't done the work in time.*

You can adapt that simple process to get to the real, root meaning of a bland adjective. But this time, use the 5 Hows.

For example, 'friendly' isn't exactly wrong for a tonal value, but it certainly isn't differentiating. So, use the 5 Hows to get beyond the superficial and keep digging until you find something unique which can be used by your writers to make your brand voice more engaging.

Working with someone who knows the brand voice well, here's how your conversation might go, with you asking the questions:

I see 'friendly' is one of the brand voice's tonal values. How is it 'friendly'?
Well, I see our brand as being like a really friendly mate.

How is it like a mate?
Well, you know, like a mate that's always willing to help.

(Already that's more differentiated. But keep gently probing.)

How come it's always willing to help?
Well, erm, it's really good at understanding your problems.

(This is good...but there's more there.)

How does it manage to be so good at understanding?
You know, the thing is, as a brand, we really listen to our customers.

(Oh dear, this was all so promising. We've hit another patch of soul-sucking bland quicksand. Keep going.)

How can it be so good at listening to our customers?
Well, the thing is, we've been around so long that we can listen because we've seen these situations before, and we're pretty good at giving exactly the right advice.

Oh, so it's friendly, but in a really insightful way. And it shares those insights. And our customers feel listened to and just 'better' because they know they're dealing with a really experienced expert?
Gosh, how did you get all that?

You might not be able to change 'Friendly' as one of the official tonal values, but by asking the 5 Hows, you've managed to unpack a bland value and turn it into something that's true for your brand and is also highly differentiating.

Your writer, working away late on a Thursday evening, will then have a lot more to work with.

> **DIG DEEPER INTO BLAND TONAL VALUES, AND YOU'LL FIND YOUR DIFFERENCE**

Chapter 18

Same territory? Different tone

In industries like banking or energy supply, there are few significant product differences. Gas is gas. An account offering 0.25% interest is exactly as interesting as another account offering 0.25% interest.

And where there are any differences, in this fast-moving world, most of those differences will be copied. Fast.

In those kinds of undifferentiated industries, if the personality that your brand is projecting isn't starkly different, then you're standing for the same thing and talking about it in the same way. Which means you're in a low-price war.

In big corporate institutions and other organisations such as the police and the church, finding a personality for the voice is even more important. The graph which shows people's trust in institutions over time slants down to the right, steep and fast. People see these institutions as untrustworthy not just because of their failures but because the way they speak to people sounds like they're comfortable being big, impenetrable, and inhuman.

The new Challenger banks out there realised this, and their tones of voice were designed to contrast strongly with the established banks. They talked about simplicity, and they talked about simplicity with a simplifying tone.

Their voices also talked about ease of use, and so tones were relaxed, informal – contrasting with the patriarchal voice that remains with the big banks.

All of these neobanks had touches of rebellion in their voices, some more than others, and optimism was a recurring tone. But some differentiated themselves by being direct and short and to the point (they're on a mission, they don't have time to stop and explain); others were more expansive (they're on a mission and need to stop and convert people along the way).

So, although all of them were challenging the status quo, often in very similar ways, and they all shared a worldview that big banks had been exploiting customers for too long, they all found their own, different voices to create a personality and express this.

In the UK's energy market, there are also some fast-growing Challenger brands. But even within the Challenger sector, there's another subdivision: companies providing energy from renewable sources. Bulb, Ovo, and Octopus share a view of the better world they want to create, but the different personalities of their voices differentiate them.

Bulb's brand Tone of Voice reflects its position as the UK's biggest green energy supplier: it's frank and logical ('for every unit you use, we make sure a unit is produced and put on the grid by a renewable source').

Ovo takes a rabble-rousing tone, starting scary by saying, 'We're all worried about the climate crisis' and then adopting a team-making tone ('together we can fight it') before trying to be jolly at the end: 'This means that just by joining us you'll be restoring nature and cutting carbon – about 1 tonne of it a year!'

Octopus Energy's narrative has a straightforward approach – they assume that you know what energy is and that what's guiding your decision is an aversion to some of the tactics used by the big energy suppliers in the past. Their tone is, therefore, straight-talking: 'All our tariffs feature 100% renewable electricity and no exit fees.'

All of them talk about renewable energy, all are challenging the dominant and more famous suppliers, but each of them finds a different personality for their voice.

If your customer knows they won't notice the difference when they use your product, it's a good idea to help make them feel better about who they choose by using your voice to create a different personality for your brand.

> **DIFFERENTIATING YOUR BRAND'S TONE OF VOICE IS CRITICAL IN COMMODITISED SECTORS**

Case study #3

Glint. Creating the Tone of Voice for a fintech startup.

Every Founder of a successful startup is their own particular kind of crazy. The challenge when you're creating a Tone of Voice for their brand isn't to make them seem sane. It's to make the rest of the world feel like it's lost its mind for not having seen what they've seen.

When you're doing this, having a consistent Tone of Voice is critical.

In 2016, Verbal Identity was asked to create a differentiating brand voice for a fintech startup called Glint. Glint's point of difference was that it believed money should still be backed by gold. And as 'goldbugs' (enthusiasts or believers in the eternal financial power of gold), they wanted to provide investors with a credit card where their underlying funds were backed by gold.

The joy of working with Founders of Challenger brands is that they come with a narrative for the brand and its voice. It's often the very first thing they talk to you about because they're in constant world-changing pitch mode.

So, with a strong narrative in place for Glint, we just had to find a Tone of Voice that was a natural amplification of that narrative.

We conducted conventional desk and face-to-face research with the investors, members of the founding team, and relevant journalists. We also did competitive analysis to look for other brands' voices. However, looking at conventional competitors when you're working with unconventional brands doesn't work: they don't exist.

Instead, we looked at how Challenger brands in other sectors had found their voice.

Challenger brands, like Brew Dog, often use a Tone of Voice which is confrontational and tribal. We knew this would be consistent with Glint's Challenger narrative, but we felt that people were more conservative with their money. We needed to build trust first.

We knew that Challenger brands often leveraged the mouth of their Founder, like Virgin Atlantic had done for many years with Sir Richard Branson. But we also knew that people are more willing to trust their money to an institution than an individual.

As we listened to the Founders about their mission, something stood out: they were sick of the banking system and its inbuilt unfairness to individuals. They wanted to make money fairer. This became one of the tonal values for the voice: 'fair'. It meant that they wouldn't resort to bamboozling the general readers of their copy with detailed analysis of monetary supply. Instead, they'd write to keep things simple and transparent.

They were, however, doing something technical. So, they wanted to include some sense of technicality in their voice. But should it be Ferrari-like technology or something else? To keep making money fairer, they would better represent themselves with a technical Tone of Voice which conveyed their deep knowledge and skills polished by many years of experience. With just a hint of bravery in battle.

And to allay anyone's fears, their voice needed to create a sense of safety and security. So, they'd always take time to explain how they stored gold, how they transacted, how they behaved. And they'd do it in a way that sounded steady, assured, without overpitching into salesmen's language.

The brand language of a startup is one of its earliest statements of culture. Glint's simple and direct language won fans outside of the financial community as well. The card was ranked by the women's magazine *Elle* as one of the six best bank cards.

And for a startup, brand language becomes part of the playbook.

Within a couple of years, Glint expanded and opened operations in the US.

It's also a hook for PR firms and journalists to write about you. Glint's successful growth was powered by a strong image from the visual identity team, which, along with the language, was carried around the world by the world's leading press.

THE GROUND LEVEL DETAILS: (OR, 'GET THE BASICS RIGHT, YOU FUDGING DONKEY')

Chapter 19

Ground Level Details

Once you've defined the narrative and tone of your voice, it just remains for you to define the Ground Level elements of your voice: the things that appear on the page and the things which hold it all together. These are the Nuts and Bolts of your brand voice.

This includes your lexicon: the words and phrases which are or aren't in character for your brand. Specifying the words and phrases you use or don't use saves you and your teams a lot of time.

When you're deciding your lexicon, you can choose to avoid jargon. Sometimes, though, it's useful. Tell a doctor you're suffering from tachycardia rather than saying your heart is racing, and they're likely to take you more seriously. Similarly, using the same vocabulary that your consumers do signals experience; using a set of slightly more technical jargon can signal expertise.

There are choices to be made around grammar – should you have a formal grammar or go for something a bit more conversational? (But be careful – see Chapter 51, 'Grammar is a class war'.)

And there are choices on your sentence length. If you remember Mini's copy, it had a sentence that was only three words long. While that's definitely conversational grammar, it also reflects Mini's personality of being fun and dynamic – it probably also reflects the car's ability to chop and change direction. In contrast, Ferrari's copy had a sentence that was 30 words long – clearly, it was as carefully engineered as one of their cars.

The most effective brand voices choose Ground Level Details which are a natural amplification of the narrative and the tonal value so that each level of the voice reinforces the other levels.

If your brand is trying to disrupt the world of consumers who've been sold to by the big, formal, dominant brands, your worldview probably isn't suited to a grammar that is formal and traditional. Instead, it's likely to be conversational. Shorter sentences. Then, your idea gets fired up. And as you get into it, you're happy extending your sentence lengths. Then chop it back down. As you inject what's needed. Urgency. Determination. Action.

These decisions about Ground Level Details might seem minor compared to the other levels. But I've seen a CEO go red with frustration as once again he read a piece of his company's communications where the wrong term was used to describe their product range.

And I've sat in a meeting in the New York office of a British global brand while the marketing team had a long (read 'expensive') discussion on whether they could Americanize their vocabulary.

The Ground Level Details are as important to the flavour of your writing as the herbs are to a meal. Gordon Ramsey is often portrayed as a hothead, but he cares intensely. Why? Because his diners will notice the difference. Even if they can't say exactly why a dish is bland, they'll know when it is.

And your customers might not be able to explain exactly why your copy is confusing or bland. But on some level, they'll notice when something is missing or your Ground Level Details conflict with your voice's narrative and tonal values.

So, what needs defining, and how do you go about it?

> **DEFINING YOUR GROUND LEVEL DETAILS STRENGTHENS YOUR BRAND AND SAVES YOU TIME AND TROUBLE**

Chapter 20

You and non-you

The simplest way to construct a list of words and phrases that your writers should and shouldn't use is to trawl through existing communications and create a list, then share it with people in different departments.

Write down some of the words and phrases you use and don't use in each of these categories:

- Products
- The company
- When talking about our processes
- In Customer Service
- When talking about employee policies and recruitment

Once you're done, pass the list around. Ask people to keep adding items that they know of.

Finally, put an hour aside in your calendar and look down the list. Can you spot items which don't fit your narrative or personality? If so, suggest alternatives.

Then, get the list signed off! Quick, before anyone changes their mind.

Specifying your choice of grammar is a harder conversation. Grammar was often taught in a pedantic way at school, and for most people who went through that, they don't want anyone else let off the hook lightly. But the truth is, grammar is a cultural norm, and all cultural norms morph over time. I was told never to use contractions in my writing such as 'don't' or 'we've'. But I don't know many businesses that stick to that today. That rule might hold in your company, but it makes your brand voice – and so your company – seem archaic.

The broadest choice for grammar is whether to be formal or conversational. Most modern brands adopt a conversational grammar style which reflects how conversation itself is looser today. Markers of informal grammar include the contractions of 'won't' and 'don't' but also things like sentences not needing nouns. Being short. In other words.

Some brands take things further and use what the linguists call 'markers of discourse', such as 'So,' at the start of a sentence. Some markers quickly become overused and seem knowingly, erm, cute.

Other markers which might seem too conversational, such as 'What we mean is' or 'In other words', can be used in written communications to emphasise a point.

If your writers want to show some attitude, then words such as 'frankly' and 'actually' or 'naturally' create a sense of direct conversation.

Where the writer wants to be less pushy, the occasional 'apparently' or 'we think' are often used. Though sometimes, that might carry a hint of the passive-aggressive. Wouldn't you say?

There are a couple more notes about jargon. When you specify your Ground Level Details, don't just list which jargon words your writers can use. Also specify when, and with which audiences, you use it.

Make sure you point out to your writers that they must avoid the 'curse of knowledge'. This is where you forget how much more you know than your readers do, and you forget they won't follow along easily with what you're talking about.

Finally, remember that there are moments when a small dollop of jargon is useful for showing people that you know what you're talking about, even if they don't. But hey, that's the Zeigarnik effect for you.

> **WHAT'S RIGHT IS WHAT'S RIGHT FOR YOUR BRAND AND YOUR AUDIENCE**

Chapter 21

How Mini and Ferrari carefully control the Ground Level Details of their brand voices

How did the writers at Mini and Ferrari control the Ground Level Details of their brand voices? Here's Mini's copy again:

> Born to corner. Driving a Mini is a ton of fun, thanks to its legendary go-kart handling. We could go on about its lightning-quick responses and glue-like grip…

Clearly, in the agreed lexicon of phrases to be used for Mini, you'll find 'go-kart handling'. (You might even find a note to say that 'go' and 'karting' are always hyphenated.) It's certainly used in all the brand's media channels.

Mini's writers vary their sentence lengths to create a choppy, fast-changing variety in their copy. I like to think that this is a clever psychological trick, as the copy echoes the experience of driving a Mini. Being able to chop and change gear. Braking. Accelerating away fast.

The Mini brand voice also uses what my English teacher would've called the first-person plural: 'We'. When the writer acknowledges their authorial hand in the copy's creation, it immediately makes the copy seem less formal.

Even in a short piece of copy like this, there are choices about grammar, another Ground Level element. The first sentence, 'Born to corner', isn't a complete sentence in the traditional definition as it lacks a noun (the person or thing which was born).

I can imagine a conversation between a writer and a CMO where the CMO might be a stickler for complete and legitimate sentences. And the writer isn't. If they've built agreement in advance about why they should adopt an informal, twenty-first-century grammar, then that conversation can be brief.

Here's Ferrari's copy again.

> The Ferrari Roma embraces the Side Slip Control 6.0 concept, which incorporates an algorithm that delivers a precise estimate of sideslip to the onboard control systems. The SSC 6.0 integrates systems such as the E-Eff, F1-Trax, SCM-E Frs, and Ferrari Dynamic Enhancer, the latter debuting in the Race Position on the Ferrari Roma. The aim of the 5-position manettino is to make the Ferrari Roma's handling and grip even more accessible by extending the setting ranges thanks to the introduction of the Race position.

One of the most striking things about any piece of Ferrari copy is its liberal use of jargon words. Not many people know what 'E-Eff, F1-Trax, SCM-E Frs' are, but the copywriters use it without explaining it, assuming that the reader shares their knowledge. Which is probably why they've done it that way.

Words like 'algorithm' aren't unfamiliar to most readers, but again they are sophisticated words which are rarely used in everyday conversation. There's been some choice by Ferrari's writers to make sure they're using words which maintain a serious formality. Where Mini's copy seems like an invitation to get into a conversation with the brand, Ferrari's copy seems like an engineer's lecture.

Part of that effect is created by Ferrari's choice of sentence length. All of the sentences are more than 20 words long. One big sentence hammers you after another.

Ferrari's writers carefully engineered subclauses using commas, a grammatical choice implying a sophisticated writer and, probably, therefore, a sophisticated reader.

Neither Mini nor Ferrari's copy uses swear words or references to deities, but Ferrari does seem to have its own sacred worship of materials, mentioning them as frequently as possible.

> **STRONG BRAND VOICES HAVE DIFFERENTIATED GROUND LEVEL DETAILS**

Chapter 22

A short note on short sentences

Varying the length of your sentences can build a mesmerising rhythm. From the way you wrap a reader in an extended sentence with a carefully constructed metaphor. To bringing them up short.

But it's also worth thinking about the maximum length of your sentences.

The American Press Institute studied what effect sentence length has on comprehension. Here's what they found[1] when they rewrote a newspaper article by varying the average sentence length.

At eight words, readers understand all your text.

Even eleven-word sentences are easy for your readers to understand.

---

[1] Source: 'Readers' Degree of Understanding,' American Press Institute. The research, based on studies of 410 newspapers, correlated the average number of words in a sentence with reader comprehension.

But then, when you extend your average sentence length to 21 words, your readers increasingly lose their way in the thickets.

At 43 words, the average readers' comprehension wavers as they have to wade through your extended thought, which probably has lots of subclauses and ramblings, leaving them remembering only a little and comprehending less than 10%, which isn't very good news at all.

Eight words: 100%

43 words: 9%

What to do?

The next time you're writing and you find that one of your sentences goes over two lines, it's probably too long. Stop. There is more than one idea in that long sentence. See if you can break the sentence up into its individual ideas. Say what relates to what. And what else relates to what else in another sentence.

You'll keep your reader for longer.

The curse of all style guidance is that the writer inevitably breaks their own rules. I'm sure I have. But I excuse myself on the basis that this is guidance, not rules. And I'm sure I had a good excuse when I did it.

> **SHORT SENTENCES WIN**

Chapter 23

How car brands, governments, and destinations use Ground Level Details

When thinking is free and everything else costs money, isn't it worth thinking about what a change in your lexicon can do to add value to your brand?

Travel, leisure, and destination brands are very good at using the Ground Level Details to signal greater value.

I remember walking through an airport after a long flight and seeing a sign for 'Executive Showers' – how I'd have loved a proper executive shower rather than any old shower. I'm sure if you had two entrances to the showers and put a sign saying 'Showers' over one and 'Executive Showers' over the other, you could charge more for people coming in one side than the other.

Restaurants do it as well. I remember in the early hipster days of working in Shoreditch in London, there were a few brave outposts of eating. One place served a glorified English breakfast with the menu offering 'two pan-fried eggs'. They sounded so much cooler than fried eggs. Though I never thought what else you could use to fry eggs – slippers?

There is a theory that each time you add an adjective to the description of one of your dishes on your menu, you can add another 10% to its price.

Travel brands work hard on their lexicon, emphasising that you should pay a few hundred pounds more for a 'fully flat bed' compared to just a 'flat bed'. My friend Dan swears that a strip club near LAX airport was going bust until some genius had the idea of changing the sign outside from 'Nude Table Dancing' to 'Fully Nude Table Dancing'. Nude is nude. But fully nude has even fewer clothes than no clothes at all.

(There's also a joke that local organic supermarkets don't have 'five items or less' above their speedy checkout, but 'five items or fewer', just to prove that you're in the right kind of place to pay all this money.)

Most governments fall into the trap of thinking that brand guidelines and style guides are the same thing. They'll often have a 40-page document which shows the different ways you can (and can't) treat the visual elements, but there'll be only one page of guidance on the Tone of Voice. But just as brands need to communicate in order to persuade people, governments are also in a battle to win attention, trust, and loyalty.

If you're creating the guidelines for a government or large corporation, the temptation is to try to maintain authority with an unsmiling austere voice. Yet, at the same time, the government leaders are working hard to appear more human and personable.

This dissonance often creates distrust as people feel they're being asked to believe in one thing, but when they get to reading the practical details, the personality has been only a front.

But it doesn't have to be this way. That same severity of emotional control used to be the dominant Tone of Voice for airlines' inflight safety videos. The thinking was, perhaps, that you had to use an authoritative tone to make people pay attention. And then along came Air New Zealand, who realised you won more minds and hearts by having a Tone of Voice that was more human.

> **EVERY ORGANISATION, AND EVERY KIND OF ORGANISATION, NEEDS TO DEFINE ITS GROUND LEVEL DETAILS**

Case study #4

A BIG 4 UK SUPERMARKET IS GENIUS WITH ITS LEXICON

The Customer Service Director of one of the UK's four biggest super-markets was waiting to step into the lift and go home for the evening. When the doors opened, the CEO stepped out, saw him, and said, 'I hope you're not going to give me another one of those useless word clouds for the next Board meeting'.

So, the Customer Service Director turned on his heel, went back to his desk, and called us.

What started out as a project to understand customers' experiences in-store ended up showing what language could do for the brand. In particular, it revealed the value of making the right choices in your Ground Level Details.

In the early stages of the project, we were running software to analyse the huge amount of unstructured data in the 100,000 customer surveys that were completed each month.

Structured data is easy to process: it's the tick boxes where you indicate whether you thought the store was very clean/clean/OK/dirty/very dirty.

Unstructured data is harder to process, because it's the moment when the customer is allowed to talk free-form – and talk free-form about whatever they want.

A word cloud is sometimes used, but when it meets a sentence like, 'You used to have a lot of mess in the store but now you've cleared up the mess, I can reach the avocados which are never ripe, and I'll never shop with you again', it just thinks the customer is really interested in 'mess'. (And you'll be surprised by the number of different ways people can spell 'aisles'.)

The software we'd found was very good at analysing the themes behind the customer's response. It quickly identified that the biggest single cause of frustration was interaction with a staff member. In particular, 'The girl was rude'.

The Customer Service Director was delighted – he could pitch the Board to fund a politeness campaign.

He asked us, as super-specialists in language, how he should go about that.

We told him that as super-specialists in language, we knew the interesting part of 'The girl was rude' wasn't 'rude' but 'the girl'.

'The girl' is a pejorative term in everyday English. Think of 'The Girl with the Pearl Earring'.

Shoppers thought of the team members as low-level, untrained, uninformed skivvies.

Yet the staff had an average of twelve years' experience, were trained regularly and knew a lot about the produce.

If language was going to do anything, it should help change shoppers' perception of the staff's level of expertise.

The Customer Service Director was even more pleased now.

He asked us how we'd do it.

We recommended that the supermarket change the team members' name badges.

'Like how?' he asked.

'Well, if they've got twelve years' service, why not put that on there...or if they're Head of the Dairy section, you could call them "Head of Dairy".'

'I like that', he said.

But we hadn't finished.

'Or you could even call them "Dairy Genius".'

And he laughed, 'I see what you've done there, Chris. You've stretched it to the breaking point to show how we could go too far. No one would do that.'

'Ah', I replied. 'Maybe someone would. Pull out your phone.' He pulled out the latest iPhone.

'If your phone goes wrong, where do you take it? Who tells you what to do to fix it?'

'An Apple...Genius. At the Genius Bar'.

Exactly. Even a small adjustment in the Ground Level Details can help add huge amounts of value to a brand.

MAKING YOUR VOICE CONSISTENT AND FLEXIBLE

Chapter 24

Flexing your brand voice

Imagine you have a great friend who's a joker. You know you can count on them to see the funny side of any situation. They'll always make a joke about it. What a friend. What a blessing.

One day, you hear that you need to go to a funeral. You can't face going on your own. Are you going to take that friend with you?

Come on, why not? They're a good friend.

Oh, because they're *always* joking. Because you can *always* count on them to see the funny side – even when there really isn't a funny side, and they can't stop making jokes about it.

And what if your brand can never change its tone? Simply, your customers won't take it with them as often as you'd like.

Consistency is essential. But consistency doesn't mean unchanging: it means your brand voice also needs to know how to adapt its tone to suit any channel or situation: social media jokes as well as sincere Customer Service apologies, a brand-building exercise, and a money-off flash sale.

This is where the writers can play with the tonal values: turning one or two up while turning another one or two down. You never completely lose any of the tonal values; you just adjust them to suit the situation.

Imagine you're the CMO or CXO of a Challenger bank. Everyone is now agreed that the tonal values of your brand voice are 'Ambitious', 'Positive', and 'Welcoming'.

(That's part of the description of one of the UK's most successful Challenger banks, by the way, but this scenario is not based on anything that happened to them. We're only borrowing their tonal values to make a point.)

One afternoon, you're given a new Customer Service letter to sign off. It has to go out before 5 p.m., apologising for a recent outage. And one of your writers, somewhere, mentioning no names (but really, Ryan!) has messed up.

The draft of the letter starts by saying how glad you are that the customer's with you on this 'journey'. And you're sure that if they could just be more positive, you're gonna completely smash the whole UK banking scene.

It's 4.55 p.m. The letter needs to go out in the next five minutes. Will you sign it off?

It's certainly consistent with the brand's worldview. And it's consistent with the tonal values of Ambition, Positivity, and being Welcoming. But yes, you're right, those values are overwhelming any other feelings. Like empathy.

Now imagine instead that you had time to point out to the writer that they seem to have turned all the tonal values 'up to 11'.

Ryan comes back with a new draft of the letter. It now says that the bank is sorry. And it will endeavour to avoid critical deficiencies in service functionalities henceforth.

Happy now?

Ryan's thrown away the chance to use the brand to create engagement and value. He did it by turning all the tonal values down to zero.

So, you ask Ryan to put 'Welcoming' back in, add a small dollop of 'Ambitious', and can he now be stronger on 'Positive'?

This time, Ryan comes back with a letter which says you appreciate the fact that the customer contacted you about the outage, and you're sorry it happened. You will always welcome their comments and criticisms. You'd like to help fix the problem. You are one of the leading UK Challenger banks, but this kind of thing won't help you continue to lead the field, and it certainly won't help your customer. And then you let them know how you'd like to make good.

Would you sign the letter now?

And how could you brief your writers to flex the voice to suit the situation each time?

> **YOUR BRAND VOICE NEEDS TO FLEX TO SUIT HUNDREDS OF DIFFERENT SITUATIONS**

Chapter 25

Turn up the bass. The in-laws are gone

Here are some situations where you'll need to flex your brand's voice:

- You're writing an internal memo about a competition at your company.
- Your company's just won an industry award, and you want to talk about it on LinkedIn.
- There's been backlash about a new project – you have to write a blog post addressing it.
- A journalist is interviewing you about how your brand systematises innovation.
- You need to make a short video about your new diversity policy.
- You have to post to TikTok to show your fun-lovin' side.
- You have to post on LinkedIn to hire a new intern to the marketing team.

Throughout, you want to make your brand voice reflect the situation it's in, while always reinforcing the brand's values.

How can you do it?

Have you ever owned a 'HiFi separates system'? No? A bit too 1989? All right, did you ever mix music yourself on some desktop software? Right, we're talking about the same thing, basically.

You have little sliders which control the different frequency ranges in the music. You can adjust each range from 1 to 10.

There are moments when you want to drop out any high tones and get the bass thumping through.

And there are moments, such as when the in-laws are visiting, where you want to drop the bass and push up those mids and highs, to let Danielle de Niese's voice shine through.

You can do the same with your brand voice. You can turn the different tonal values up and down to make the voice flex to fit different situations.

In the Customer Service letter from the last chapter, you realised that 'Welcoming' shouldn't be as strong in that situation, so you turned it down. You wanted to remind your customer how Ambitious your bank is, but you didn't want to come off as cavalier about what you've just put them through, so you took it down a little. You realised you needed to make good and be seen to be doing something about it – so you turned Positive up much higher.

You can help your writers by asking them to adjust the tonal values like they'd adjust a Graphic Equaliser (EQ). You can help them more by working through a few recurring situations, showing them the Graphic EQ settings for each.

The important thing to remember is that you never turn any tonal value off completely and you never turn everything up to 10.

Some brand teams even go as far as including the Graphic EQ device, filled in with a set of adjusted tonal values, on every brief.

You can draw up a template with a slider, 1 to 10, for each of your brand voice's tonal values. Then, as an exercise, give it to your writers and ask them to draw in the levels for each of the scenarios at the start of this chapter. You might not all agree on each value, you might provoke a hearty discussion. But you'll certainly be reminding them of your tonal values and how the writers can think about adjusting them for each situation.

> **GET YOUR TEAM TO DRAW UP THE GRAPHIC EQ FOR EACH NEW SITUATION**

Chapter 26

Flex the voice to build loyalty

One of the most frustrating things about my school days was when I was in the sixth form, and I was still called 'West' by the teachers. I don't know if it was ever a good, human, nurturing idea to call someone by their surname, but after seven years, it certainly had no appeal left in it for me.

I was 18, I could drink in pubs (legally), I could vote, go off to war, and these people who'd known me for seven years hadn't flexed their Tone of Voice to me at all.

I used to think: you know me, I know you. What hierarchy are you desperately trying to support by maintaining that way of speaking to me, pretending that we haven't built up some kind of relationship over these years? Needless to say, when I was free to leave that school, I never went back. I had no sense of a relationship that had developed or been recognised, and so I felt no loyalty.

Ridiculous.

Except that's exactly how most brand copywriters are told to treat their customers.

If you've been with a traditional bank for 20 years, the way they speak to you after that time is the same way they spoke to you at the beginning. There's no flexing of the tone over time.

Now, I realise that when brand directors are struggling to maintain consistency in their brand voice, asking them to write something else that's consistent but also flexible is a big ask.

But some kind of signalling is worth it. And many brands – in different situations – do manage it. The Tone of Voice from British Airways to its Bronze Card holders is not as flattering as the Tone of Voice to its Gold Card holders, that's for sure.

It's worth it because every relationship has its bumps in the road. At those moments, customers decide whether to stick it out or chuck it in. Surely, one of the things that influence them is the awareness of the time they've invested in the relationship – that's why long-term customers feel more affronted when normal service breaks down. But if the time of the relationship has been recognised regularly by the brand, using a tone that matures over time to imply greater closeness and loyalty, then surely, it's harder to break up from the brand.

Surely, it's also easier for the customer to feel that if they reach out to the company, it won't be a company-style reaction but a more personable response.

It's relatively easy to flex the voice to reflect the relationship. Certainly, you can introduce stock phrases, such as 'After all this time, we're glad we're still your preferred bank.'

But you can also make the grammar less formal. You can specify to your writers that they change the Graphic EQ's relative values.

It's starting to happen on Customer Service calls, where the person at the contact centre now asks if it's 'OK to call you Chris'.

Perhaps it's time to introduce some of that thinking into how the brand writes in other communications to specific customers.

> **HOW BRANDS SPEAK TO THEIR CUSTOMERS REVEALS HOW MUCH THEY VALUE THAT RELATIONSHIP**

Chapter 27

An exercise to be more flexible

No tennis player gets better at playing matches just by playing long games of tennis. Instead, they have drills and exercises to work on specific skills or build muscle sets. You can do the same for your writing team's skills and writing muscles.

This exercise takes around 90 minutes, and all the usual workshop rules apply: there are no 'wrong answers', sharing work with others helps people learn from each other, and because this is an exercise, we're not trying to be 'right'. We're trying to push the boundaries and work the muscles in the extreme.

(The other important rule for workshops is, of course, don't think the learning ends when the workshop ends: send through two or three emails in the following weeks which refocus people's minds on what they've learned and show recognition to people who are already doing well.)

This exercise is called Dial. For each of your brand's tonal values, imagine it's on a dial which you can turn down to 1 and all the way up to 10. For 1, 4, 7, and 10 on the dial, pick a well-known movie character or public figure that represents the strength of that emotion.

For example, we were working with the John Lewis Partnership, the famous UK retailer, who wanted to help their e-com team flex their voice. One of the tonal values was 'Confidence', so we plotted the dial with Rex from *Toy Story* at 1 (he's going for fearsome, but just not feeling it). At 4, we had Piglet from *Winnie the Pooh*. Piglet is loving and caring, but struggling to have the confidence just to accept himself.

At 7, we had Velma from *Scooby-Doo* – someone who occasionally displays a strong confidence that allows them to take charge (ordering Shaggy to 'March!').

At 10, we had President Trump (whose statements included 'All of the women on *The Apprentice* flirted with me – consciously or unconsciously. That's to be expected.').

We asked each person coming to the workshop to bring a piece of copy with them that they were working on at the time, and one piece that had been challenging or hard when they had first written it.

We explained the dial and then divided the room up into teams who worked on a piece of copy between them for one particular space on the dial. We asked them to rewrite it through the voice of the character at that position: Rex, Piglet, Velma, or President Trump.

They had 15 minutes, picked one piece of copy, and worked on it while other teams worked on their piece of copy at their position on the dial.

When time was up, they read their pieces back, often to big laughs, and then moved to the next position on the dial and repeated it.

As the exercise progressed, each team realised how they could turn 'Confidence' up or down.

But they also got better at pushing the boundaries for each position on the dial.

At the end, we asked the room where they thought their brand voice should pitch its level of confidence, and I'm glad to say they were at Velma, rather than Rex or President Trump.

A week later and again a week after that, they came back together to practise the other tonal values, using the Dial exercise.

GROW YOUR WRITERS' SKILLS BY GETTING THEM TOGETHER EVERY MONTH TO LEARN SOMETHING NEW

Chapter 28

Why cookery books are more than just a list of ingredients

Why are good cookery books so helpful?

Why is Net-a-Porter's copy so readable?

It's all to do with using smarter message structures.

With a good cookery book, each recipe is easy to follow. Often, you'll be given a description of how delicious the dish is, which inspires you to make it. Then the author talks about the ingredients you need. And finally, they'll tell you how to cook it. Every page is constructed the same way.

Net-a-Porter's product copy also has its own structure. It starts by telling you a little about the designer's ethos and the materials. Then it'll tell you something about the product details. Brilliantly, it always finishes by suggesting ways you can accessorize the item or suggesting other things you can wear with it to make it uniquely yours. Every product description feels fresh, but they're all constructed the same way.

When you're trying to produce very high volumes of copy every day (for example, in retail, where your writers can be expected to create 50 or more pieces of copy), you can save time by designing a framework and asking your writers to fit content to it. Some writers might object. Until it's 7 p.m., and they've only done a fifth of the work required.

Smart message structures are one of the most effective Ground Level Details for saving time (and, therefore, money).

For the writers, it's great not to be battling trying to decide what goes where. But they can also use frameworks at the briefing stage, using each item in the framework as a checklist to make sure they have all the information they'll need to do their job.

For example, with Vauxhall, we defined their message structure to have four clear sections following one after another:

The first part was 'Look what you can do' – we wanted to remind potential customers that although the Vauxhall brand was very familiar to them, they might not realise how technologically sophisticated the car was. A good way of opening was to talk about a benefit, something they'd be able to do, preferably by relating it back to an insight into the customer's life.

The next stage pointed out which of the car's features enabled you to do this.

Next, the writer needed to dive into the technology just a bit, to prove that the car was more sophisticated than most people assumed.

Finally, the message structure encouraged the writer to wrap up by talking about some of the other benefits.

Of course, not all copy fits into regular-shaped boxes like retail and e-commerce. But even when your communications can splurge out, defining a message structure stops them from splurging out too much.

Many writers will know the AIDA framework for structuring copy: start with something Attention-grabbing, something that will make the reader want to read what you've written.

Once you have their attention, deepen their Interest by expanding on the offer or problem you mentioned, and show you have a solution. Then, build emotional and rational Desire for your particular solution. Finally, be very clear about what Action you want the reader to take now.

Once you've defined the voice, learnt how to flex it, and constructed your timesaving frameworks, it's time to think about pulling it all together into guidelines that people will use every day.

DEFINING A STRUCTURE FOR YOUR MESSAGES SAVES TIME AND MONEY

Case study #5

OnStar. How to use the Graphic EQ to switch from saving
someone's life one minute to offering coffee discounts the next.

OnStar is an in-car 'safety and help' communications system fitted to General Motors' cars. When you're driving and need directions to a new destination or need to refuel (you or your car), you simply press a button, and you're instantly connected to a well-trained member of staff. Explain what you want, and they download directions to your car or book you a hotel. In an emergency, if you're stuck or have had an accident, you can press the button, and the team will call emergency services and stay talking with you until they arrive. The safety sensors in the system will also detect a crash, and if you don't respond to the call from the contact centre, they'll scramble the emergency services out to your exact location.

It's more than helpful; it could save your life. And as Rebecca Lawman, OnStar's European Marketing Director at the time, pointed out to us, that's the challenge. Having a monolithic brand voice wouldn't work.

The communications in advertising, CRM, and different channels need to flex from truly life-and-death situations to regular announcements about system upgrades, money-off vouchers, and subscription renewals.

This was a good moment for the Graphic EQ.

The first stage of the work was to create with the team a full definition of the brand's voice across all three levels. Even this wasn't straightforward. The voice of the brand had originally been established in the US. But this brought advantages and disadvantages.

The advantages were obviously that the brand's values had already been established.

The disadvantage was that there could have been a temptation to just apply that US definition of the brand voice to the European market.

Luckily, the UK brand team immediately saw that since they were involved in delicate communications with their drivers, it was important to match the voice to the UK market exactly.

It's in moments like this that having a narrative for the brand voice becomes valuable: it makes sure that when you adapt the voice for a new market, it will stay within the territory of the brand and its values.

Although a Brand Voice Narrative wasn't an explicit part of the original guidelines, we were able to effectively reverse engineer it from the original Tone of Voice values.

Now that we had the voice's territory set, we could look at how the original Tone of Voice values should be mapped to the UK market. Fortunately, the original Tone of Voice values were more than just 'four adjectives on a page', and this helped us to find comparable UK values and unpack each with 50 words.

The final challenge then was to make clear how the voice flexed for different situations. This was when the Graphic EQ became supremely useful.

We started by identifying more than 20 different situations where the brand needed to communicate and mapped a 'driver state' for each. However, each situation isn't a 'one and done' communication, but needed an evolving dialogue from problem to resolution, so we also mapped the driver's evolving emotional state in each situation.

We worked with the brand team to map the Graphic EQ's values for the brand voice in each situation and each channel.

For any situation, the writers could then script dialogue cues that were perfectly matched to the emotional need of the driver but remain consistent with the overall brand voice. In simple situations such as hotel bookings, this was straightforward. In life-saving situations, this was more complex.

Throughout, though, the brand voice was maintained. This wasn't just for 'brand equity' reasons. It meant that the customer was reassured by a consistent brand and a consistent experience.

At the end of our work, there was a brand voice which was relevant for the UK market but which reflected the US parent brand values.

The brand team members were aligned on the voice and confident in using it every day.

Finally, they were comfortable flexing the voice for each of the different situations they faced.

CREATING LASTING CHANGE

Chapter 29

Everything you need in your brand voice guidelines

Once you've defined your brand voice, how to flex it, and created your timesaving frameworks, it's time to capture everything you've developed in new guidelines.

Sometimes, brand voice guidelines are standalone. Sometimes, they're integrated into bigger brand identity guidelines. Either way, they need to define the three levels of the voice and several other things for your writers and nonwriters:

The intro letter from the CEO. This is best as a 100-word note on the value of your brand and the value to the business of everyone speaking with one voice.

Why the new voice has been defined. This is usually a 200-word introduction from the CMO or CXO, explaining what the voice can do for everyone, and why the voice has evolved. It should also acknowledge how the new brand voice fits in with other brand projects that have gone before.

A reminder of the brand's values. This reminds people how the voice is there to amplify the brand's values.

The new positioning of our voice vs. our competitors'. Show how you differ from your competitors and maybe talk about how your brand voice is similar to other admired brands from outside your category. If possible, illustrate these differences and similarities with one or two simple graphs, picking one of your values for each axis.

10,000 ft: the narrative of the voice. Explain why a brand voice is important. Be clear on the three parts of it: we want [this kind of world], we are [this kind of people], and stand against [that]. Include examples of where your Brand Voice Narrative is already strong. Compare your Brand Voice Narrative with other brands'.

1,000 ft: Tone of Voice/personality. Always more than just four insipid adjectives, it's a unique collection of three to four adjectives which describe your voice and make it highly differentiated. Each tonal value is carefully unpacked in a 25–50-word description, and together, the tonal values create a personality that expresses your Brand Voice Narrative.

In this section, help people understand the brand voice personality by citing real people, movie characters, or other brands which strongly demonstrate each of those values and explain how they embody that personality trait in their language. Include lots of examples from those people who show that tonal value at work.

Ground Level: the Nuts and Bolts of how your brand voice is put together. Along with the words and phrases you do and don't use, grammar, jargon, and sentence lengths, include some style choices (such as how you handle abbreviations), and say which dictionary is your reference source.

The Graphic Equaliser. Introduce the concept and include examples to show how the tonal values are adjusted for different moments.

Message Structure. Explain how it makes life simpler. Be clear it can apply to all messages, long or short. Give lots of examples.

Our voice in one memorable sentence. You're asking people to remember a lot. Help them by giving them a single sentence which memorably sums up your brand voice.

Before and After examples of your new brand voice in action. We've found that a minimum of five examples from each of the key product lines, geographies, and target markets is essential for turning theory into practice.

Writers' tips. Include a section on basic grammar and a note on tricky words that often cause confusion. Spend some time making writers' lives easier with a few tips on how to imagine the person they're writing for, writing one-to-one rather than broadcasting to many, and how to find inspiration. (We've included some writers' tips in Chapter 56.)

> **AN INTRODUCTION FROM THE CEO ENCOURAGES PEOPLE TO START USING THE BRAND VOICE.**
> **PRACTICAL TIPS AT THE END PERSUADE THEM IT'S EASY TO DO**

Chapter 30

Sticking plasters can't fix a broken leg

Most of us only consider the brand voice at moments of peak frustration. For example, you want to launch a new product, and suddenly the writing team just can't capture the product's spirit. Or a competitor's launch has disrupted the market, and you can't seem to find the voice to own the centre ground anymore.

How can language, that wonderful thing we've all been doing since childhood, be so hard? Especially when other departments seem able to get difficult things to happen, like building new prototypes or launching complex software or getting new pricing agreements in place.

When there's a crisis, it's genuine, but it feels like it'll only be temporary.

So, in the heat of the crisis, you hire an expensive freelance writer who has a particular style and get them to churn through the project and write some key copy.

Or you decide to stay later each evening and write it yourself until this burst of writing is done.

But while the crisis was temporary, the underlying cause wasn't. And there's another crisis coming along. After all, brand language is working everywhere, all the time.

So, when the next crisis hits, you're tempted to add another temporary writer or two.

But soon, the cost of hiring temporary writers is taking a bite out of your budget. Or you're now writing a large chunk of the copy yourself, which means you're not focussing on the real value-add parts of your job. Instead, you're in the office at 9 p.m. on a Thursday night, while all the writers have gone down the pub.

Even worse, a couple of months later, the sticking plaster comes off. And while you were originally credited for fixing the crisis, you're now credited with investing in a temporary solution that has cost money and hasn't changed anything. That's not what you were hired for.

Very few CMOs or CXOs have the luxury of building a brand voice from zero with no baggage and no ghosts lurking in the corridors.

And sometimes, we have no choice but to use a temporary fix. Always though, it's a good idea to try and fix things in a sustainable way.

Of course, that's easier said than done. Where do you find the budget for that?

One of the temptations is to think that working through a crisis is enough. But as competitors become more agile, society and culture are evolving faster than ever; brand language now has to move faster than ever before, just to stay up to date and to keep engaging customers.

To make your brand voice a long-term, highly effective brand asset, it's important you help people understand its value.

It's time to think about the commercial rationale of changing your brand voice.

> **YOUR COMPANY HAS AN EVER-INCREASING NEED FOR GOOD, CLEAR ON-BRAND WRITING**

Chapter 31

Finding the money to change your brand voice

The single hardest part of any transformation program, one which produces sustained commercial benefit, is moving beyond the initial Quick Wins. Sometimes, you run out of budget; sometimes, it's professional capital that runs dry. Most often, the relief at getting any change in place – and the mental effort you've spent getting there – means it feels more rational to bank your gains and move on to improving something else.

But to move beyond those Quick Wins which anyone could have achieved, you need to win senior-level sponsorship. Which means you need to produce a robust commercial rationale for change.

But while it's easy to see the appeal of doubling the speed of your widget production at no extra cost, no one believes that writers and other creative types can be optimised in the same way.

But you can create a commercial rationale with quantifiable measures (and qualitative support) for changing the brand voice.

There are more complex measures than those which we use. But by being relatively easy, and being seen as 'reasonable', these calculations are quick to produce and win support for.

First, the quantifiable measures.

Start by taking a look at the ongoing cost of revising work. Gather together a broad sample of 100 pieces of your team's written work from the last twelve months from across all of your channels. Find out how many of those pieces were signed off in Version 1.

Then, for the pieces which weren't signed off in Version 1, find out the total number of times each of those pieces had to be rewritten *after* Version 1 was rejected.

Say your writing teams were doing well, and 85 pieces were signed off in Version 1. Congrats. But for the remaining 15 pieces, perhaps each one had to be rewritten and rewritten, with a total number of 45 rewrites.

So, for every 100 finally successful versions of copy, there are 45 unsuccessful versions being written.

With this quick estimate, you can see that $45/(85 + 45) = 35\%$ of your writing team's time is being wasted on writing the wrong thing.

Then simply multiply your total cost of all writers (salary + overheads) by 0.35, and that's the saving you can aim for by defining your brand voice more comprehensively.

(Of course, that measurement is rough and ready. Different

types of copy don't cost the same to produce: a tweet is cheaper to produce than a press ad. So, to refine this measure, do this calculation for each separate channel.)

Another illuminating stat is to compare the wastage rates of your in-house writing teams with your agency teams.

To be more comprehensive in your estimates, don't forget to allocate the cost of your own time spent reviewing revisions. Do this by making an estimate of how long it takes you to review a piece of copy and give feedback, then multiplying that by an hourly rate for your salary.

Once you have these obvious costs taken into account, there are some hidden costs of a poorly defined brand voice that need to be calculated.

YOU MUSTN'T FORGET TO CALCULATE THE COST OF YOUR OWN TIME SPENT REVIEWING POOR WORK

Chapter 32

What else is a bad brand voice costing you?

There are other costs from having a poorly defined brand voice. They're relatively easy to calculate but are often hidden or not thought about. But they definitely impact a department's spending.

Employee churn. What is the rate of churn of employees in your writing teams? Each new recruit has three costs attached to them:

1. The cost of recruiting them.
2. The cost of onboarding them – e.g., the cost of your HR team's time to induct them, plus the new writer's time spent going through various induction requirements instead of just writing.
3. The cost of the writer being less than fully productive as they learn your brand voice. This on-ramping in companies with a clear brand voice, like Mini and Ferrari, takes about three days, but in most companies is at least three weeks. Where the brand voice isn't defined, it can easily take three months for a writer to become fully productive.

You can easily estimate the saving you'll achieve when you reduce the time it takes to onboard new writers. Make your best estimate of how long it takes each new writer to become fully productive and use that to calculate what proportion of their first year's salary is spent before being fully productive. (You should be able to reduce that to just three days with a comprehensively defined brand voice.) Then multiply by the number of new writers you hire each year.

Writer productivity. What's the difference in output between a writer who's fully engaged and one who's just not into what you do or your brand voice? It can be as much as 30%, and numerous studies have shown that as many as half of your writers can be unengaged.

(And a fifth of your team can be *actively* disengaged, which means they're not just unproductive themselves, they're actively making other people less productive. But let's take them out of the equation for now.)

The difference in productivity often comes down to how clear a direction your writers have. All good writers like clear direction, and with that, you can expect them to easily be 10% more productive. If you have that, you have a 10% saving in your total writing team's salary budget. If you don't, you're probably overspending on your writers' budget by 10%.

Freelancers. Many companies are hiring freelancers to handle overflow work at peak times. What's the cost of that? How much would you be saving if you didn't need to hire expensive contract writers? If you helped your writing team to be just 10% more productive, could you remove the need for expensive freelancers completely?

Writers' salaries. We've always found that a well-directed, enthusiastic junior-level writer is more productive than a highly paid, misdirected senior writer. With a well-defined brand voice, you can save salary costs by hiring for talent rather than experience. This is hard to calculate in practice, but what would you save if your next hire was a (well-directed) junior instead of a mid-level or senior writer?

Could you ever achieve all of those cost savings? Probably not. And even if you could, no one would believe you when you present your commercial rationale for change.

In our experience, achieving 40–50% of the total possible cost savings is a reasonable expectation over two to three years. It's probably more if you have the project skills on hand to push through all the changes. In the first year, you could easily expect to achieve 10–15% of the total possible savings.

There, of course, are also some harder to quantify costs which it's important for you to at least consider.

> **YOU CAN SAVE AS MUCH AS 25% OF YOUR WRITING TEAM'S BUDGET WHEN YOU DEFINE YOUR BRAND VOICE PROPERLY**

Chapter 33

Soft costs and hard realism

No one wants to weaken their case by including evidence that doesn't seem widely credible. However, it's important to acknowledge in some way, even if it's just to yourself, some of the less obvious costs of maintaining a badly designed brand voice.

Hypothetical costs. One of our clients told us that their writers were working three weekends every month, on average. They wondered, is there a cost that could be attributed to that?

We reasoned that their team's overtime does have a cost to the company, even if the writers aren't being paid for it. It has an impact on motivation and on how productive they can be during the rest of the week. It also has a human cost as people's relationships deteriorate or they lose physical and mental fitness.

There'd be no obvious cost saving if the team stopped having to work weekends, but their manager wanted to quantify the impact of working weekends, so we used a proxy measure.

We worked out a day rate for each person who was regularly

working weekends, and we estimated how many weekends each year each person was working. We then calculated a salary cost of this time. We didn't apply an 'overtime rate' because no one in the company was paid a different rate for working extra hours, so we knew this would weaken the case.

When we did this, the team leader was able to see that although there was no directly attributable commercial upside to the company for fixing the weekend working, each of those people was effectively paying the company a substantial amount of money each year to spend their time maintaining a poorly defined brand voice. This gave the manager the ammunition to ask for investment in new brand voice guidelines.

Qualitative impact of a poorly defined voice. There are softer values to be considered as well. Who wants to spend two-thirds of their time revising work? Who wants to be brought into work on a project solely to redo the work that took someone else three months, simply because no one could tell the original writer what the brand voice really was?

What's the human, rather than commercial, cost of hiring someone and then letting them go a year later because they can't magically guess how the brand voice should sound? Not just to the person who's thrown out quickly, but also to the feelings of insecurity of the people who've seen the hire-and-fire culture develop around them?

What's the human cost of someone who *does* get the voice, spending the outbound flight of their holiday finishing copy because there's no one else who understands the voice?

What happens if the star writer doesn't come into work one

day because they're suffering from stress? And that day turns into a month?

How much would the company slow down if your great writers, who intuitively 'get' the voice, leave to work for someone else? Someone like a competitor?

None of these have a direct cost that you can quantify easily. But they're part of the rationale for why change should happen.

Another critical part of creating the rationale for change is to identify where you can achieve positive improvements in your brand voice's effectiveness. To do this, we always recommend starting with an audit.

> **THE TRUE COST OF A POORLY DEFINED BRAND VOICE IS HOW UNPRODUCTIVE YOUR WRITING TEAM CAN BECOME**

Chapter 34

Urgent and critical

The commercial rationale described in the last three chapters will help you build a picture of how expensive it is to maintain a poorly defined brand voice. But knowing where you can create positive improvements in the effectiveness of your brand voice is equally important.

The best place to start is with an audit of your current output. The purpose of this isn't to criticise. Instead, it's to identify where you can make improvements. It involves assessing the skillsets of the people involved in producing the work and the processes you're using.

A full description of the audit process would take another book. But there are some simple things you can look at:

1. Which pieces of work are quickest/cheapest to produce, and which are slowest/most expensive?
   A. What's causing the difference: skillsets, quality of briefs, or processes? Or all of them?
   B. What costs can you attribute to the impact of producing work more slowly?

2. Which pieces of work are more/less effective?
   A. Can you measure bounce rates off pages?
   B. Why are some pages more engaging than others?
   C. Can you attribute any commercial value to those bounce rates or failed outcomes?

(For example, one banking client had a 12-month savings product. Their goal was that 100% of the people whose accounts had just expired would renew and reinvest into a new 12-month savings product within a month. Only 60% of the savers were renewing within the time frame. The cost of not engaging the other 40% was easy to calculate because there was a well-defined value for each renewed account. By tracking where people were disengaging with the copy, then running A/B tests to create a more effective renewal letter, the number of people who didn't renew was halved – and this halved the revenue which was being lost.)

3. Score your written communications in different channels for three key factors: Usability, Relevance, and Amplification of your brand's values. Use a 1–5 scorecard, and accept that your results are impressionistic rather than precise.
4. Then, can you do the same thing to score your written communications against your competitors' writing?
5. Remembering that our consumers don't just consume brands in our sector, can you now score the strength of your brand voice against 'best-in-world' examples? Could you attribute any increases in revenue if you made your brand voice as strong as the 'best-in-world'?

Why aren't those figures included in the commercial rationale you built earlier? Because unfortunately, they're likely to be less credible. There's something very concrete about reducing wastage – but improving revenue always seems more fanciful when you're talking about what is essentially a reengineering program.

However, it's good to complete both exercises because a commercial rationale and the audit for change work together.

The audit for change paints a picture of what could happen when you have a more effective voice. The commercial rationale provides the reason it must happen, and so, the urgency for it to start immediately.

When you're well-armed to state your case on the commercial impact of changing the brand voice, we've found there's something better to start your presentation with than, 'I think...'

> **UNLESS YOU BUILD A SENSE OF COMMERCIAL URGENCY, NOTHING WILL HAPPEN**

Chapter 35

Kick-starting change

Giving your investors or CEO some kind of credible assessment of how the people around them are feeling about the current brand voice is critical to winning their support.

A quick and simple survey around the company helps wrap your case in something less subjective than your opinion.

So, instead of starting with 'I think', you can open with, 'Our analysis shows…' or, even better, 'What your teams have told us is that…'

You can conduct this kind of survey in a series of ten-minute chats, or you can run it via email and other internal comms tools. We generally don't use survey software because it often only allows tick-box answers, and you'll get a richer picture of what needs changing when you allow people to answer in their own words. (All the questions below can easily be adapted, however, to work for structured, tick-box answers.)

Make sure you ask a range of people: not just marketing and Customer Service but other roles and in other regions, people with different levels of seniority. When you're asking, search for both emotional and rational reactions to your company's current narrative and language.

The questionnaire doesn't need to be long. You can find out most of what you need with just seven questions:

1. How strong do you think our voice is, compared to our competitors?
2. How strong do you think our voice is, compared to the strongest companies around the world?
3. Which part of our communications do you think is the strongest and which is the least strong?
4. When people in the company write, do you think their writing reflects our company's unique values?
5. Do you think that we're spending too much time writing and rewriting?
6. How much value do you think there might be in creating a strong and differentiating brand voice?
7. What are the barriers that you think we might have when creating a differentiating, clear, engaging brand voice?

It's great, of course, to be able to present your results with some simple analysis, and you can use two simple matrices to start.

The first matrix shows where the Quick Wins are likely to be:

Increasingly difficult to implement

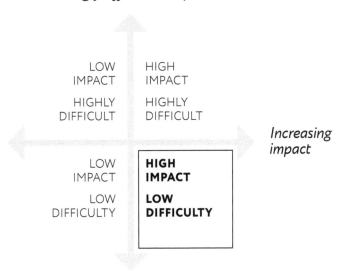

Projects which will have a high impact but aren't difficult to implement are good to start straightaway, giving you Quick Wins, erasing some people's lingering doubts, persuading more people to join you, and giving you permission to start creating more sustainable change. The issues from the top-right quadrant are equally important but will take longer.

The second matrix acknowledges the real life of the leader: some people will always be far more vocal than their importance.

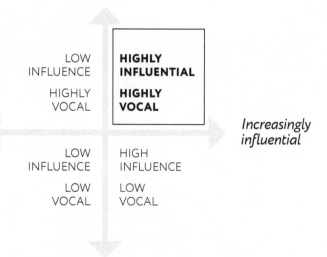

Increasingly vocal

LOW INFLUENCE	**HIGHLY INFLUENTIAL**
HIGHLY VOCAL	**HIGHLY VOCAL**
LOW INFLUENCE	HIGH INFLUENCE
LOW VOCAL	LOW VOCAL

Increasingly influential

This matrix helps to illustrate who to bring into the engagement early. It also brings up the topic that many people avoid: who should be involved in the change program?

IDENTIFY QUICK WINS TO GET THE PROJECT OFF TO A QUICK START

Chapter 36

Who should be involved in creating your new brand voice?

Short answer: everyone.

Longer answer: everyone who you can easily involve.

Why?

The biggest thing that contributes to you successfully defining your brand voice is that everyone buys into the definition and starts using it. The more people you consult along the way, the more people will feel heard and be willing to accept your recommendations.

But as a minimum, in our experience, if you don't have the following people actively involved in the research and construction of the brand voice, it won't succeed:

- Your CEO

- Your CMO
- Your CXO
- Your CFO
- The head of your sales team
- Your external agencies, such as the ad agency folk, the PR team, your packaging company, web agency, CRM agency, etc.
- The people who will be writing at 9 p.m. on a Thursday night – the writers themselves

With that many people involved, you might be worried about having to make compromises. It's rare for any project to go through without some idealistic edges being shaved off, and sometimes it feels like any kind of compromise is worth having in order to get something bought and get the train moving. And that's almost true. But the kind of compromise that isn't worth having is the one that makes it unclear exactly what you're after or exactly what you're agreeing on. While that successfully kicks the can down the street, it's usually you that'll have to pick up the dirty, bashed thing at the end.

When you're working out how to avoid too much compromise, a handy tool is the 'ARCI matrix'. When it comes to defining the brand's voice, every colleague's voice is equally valid, it's just that they don't all have the same 'voting rights'. The ARCI model helps you work out different inputs and responsibilities.

A: this is the person who is finally Accountable for the work, who signs it off. There is generally only one person who is accountable.

R: this is probably you and your immediate team, the people who are Responsible for completing the task and making decisions along the way.

C: many people are Consulted. They give input before the work can be signed off, but they don't control the output.

I: some people have to be kept Informed with things like updates on progress and the final decision, but you don't need to formally consult them or expect them to contribute to the inputs.

And always beware of the person who wasn't in the room but wanted to contribute subsequently.

If you have the support of the CEO and you find the leadership team is aligned, you might wonder whether you even need an external partner. It's a good question.

> **YOUR FINAL SUCCESS DEPENDS ON WHAT YOU DO AT THE BEGINNING**

Chapter 37

Help needed? Maybe

This section might sound self-serving. It probably is. I hope that it also offers some balance, based on experience, of when bringing in external help is a good idea and when it wouldn't be.

It is entirely possible to change the voice of your brand without any external help. In fact, there are good reasons to do it: like money. A comprehensive project for a large organisation will cost six figures. A complete set of guidelines with writer training lasting 18 months can push past six figures into seven. But there's more than just cost involved in hiring an external partner.

An external partner usually has their own methodology. You'll be expected to bend and disrupt your organisation to their method.

Few people can understand the dynamics of an organisation when they're not inside it. If you have someone that's not empathetic, then a project quickly unravels.

If you already have a generalist design agency, a specialist language consultancy might dent egos. Or offer conflicting advice. (Not wrong advice, just conflicting.)

And if you want to do it yourself, this book will help you. (This book, and an ear for language, of course.)

There are justifications for hiring an external partner or consultancy that can outweigh all of those reasons.

An outsider has an impartial view. An outsider can bring unique skills. An outsider has time to do the work while you run business as usual. And a super-specialist consultancy formed specifically to focus on just this challenge is likely to have more experience than a generalist.

What should you look for, if you decide to hire an external partner? At all costs, avoid someone who says they love your brand and can write. You need someone who understands brand strategy and understands writers, not an enthusiast.

When it's time to change your brand voice, you're looking for someone who knows how to create change. Here are some questions you can ask them:

- **How long do you think change takes?** If they say it'll take less than a year, they might be focussing on superficial change. If they say 18 months or 'Forever', then maybe they have some real experience.
- **How many people in our organisation need to change?** If their answer is less than 'everyone', then they're not seeing the whole picture. Sustained change might not happen, and then there's a danger that your professional capital will be eroded along the way.

- **Are you happy to go with the project champion's intuition, or do you think you need to dig deeper?** They need to be happy with both!
- **How do you make sure you're building cultural change rather than behavioural change?** If they look blank, then move on.

Listen to see if they are asking how this change will fit in with other changes going on now or that have taken place in the past. They need to be sensitive to this.

Avoid 'industry experts'. Industry experience is always useful, but one size never did fit all in T-shirts, and it certainly doesn't in consultancy projects. You need to outperform your sector, not be 'as good as'.

Whether you're going alone or bringing in external partners, it helps to begin with the end in mind. So, it helps to have a roadmap for the journey ahead.

> **THE VALUE OF HIRING AN EXTERNAL PARTNER IS THEIR IMPARTIALITY AND THEIR EXPERIENCE**

Case study #6

*Votary. How defining the Nuts and Bolts saved
Founders time and mental energy.*

Money is usually seen as the thing in shortest supply for a startup. But the most limiting factor is time – especially the time the Founders have available each day to do what only they can. Whenever they can delegate tasks, the time they free up for themselves can be more useful than money itself.

It used to take a number of years before the Founder would release control over language, feeling that only they can accurately express what the company stands for.

But now, the number of channels in which a brand needs to communicate has exploded. And consumers now expect to be in a dialogue with a brand that they love (rather than being the recipient of an occasional monologue). Today, the need for language has increased beyond the capability of any Founder to create it.

Having clear brand voice guidelines, then, is critical for a startup.

The two Co-founders of Votary, the UK plant-based skincare startup, realised this even before launch. And they'll admit this wasn't due to any great foresight – the need for language quickly overwhelmed them.

Already working 100 hours a week to develop and launch the brand, they needed guidelines that would let them confidently delegate the creation of content. They also needed a consistent voice which was authentically that of Arabella Preston, Co-founder, and 'face' of the brand.

Arabella's brief was precise. First, define her own voice completely, on all three levels: the narrative, the tonal values, and down to her intuitively chosen Ground Level elements. Next, create guidelines that were clear and eminently practical: with no time and not much budget, they wouldn't be able to afford to hire expensive writers for the brand.

When we researched their market, we saw that the language of skincare brands could be plotted on a graph with two axes: Individual vs. Corporate and Modern vs. Old-Fashioned.

When the leading brands' tones of voice were plotted out, it quickly became obvious that there was a clear and distinctive space which Votary could own.

The voice of boutique skincare brands tends to be that of the individual Founder, writing in the first person, using colloquialisms, and asking the reader to trust the Founder as a person.

The voice of large skincare brands focusses on explaining the science behind the product. (These voices are colder, using the third person to imply a high level of expertise in their backstory.)

We realised that Votary could claim both strengths because Arabella is a charming, personable individual and a recognised expert with strong credentials in product development. This led us to a simple, powerful idea: Votary's voice should sound like a private consultation with Arabella.

Verbal Identity had limited time with Arabella. In just two carefully constructed interview sessions, we determined the underlying narrative of how she approached developing products for their range and the key personality tones of her voice.

Throughout our conversation, we listened carefully and nudged and probed to build up a comprehensive collection of the words and phrases she'd use and not use. We were also able to build up guidelines for the other Ground Level elements, such as her use of jargon and choices around formal or informal grammar.

With their launch date approaching, and a further ramping up of demand for written content, we were able to quickly turn this research into practical guidelines. These covered how the Votary voice should sound in order to remain consistent and engaging. It also showed how the voice should 'flex' in different channels and on different occasions.

We worked side by side with the writing team to help them practice and know the voice – without the need for any heavy involvement of the Founders.

Three years after launch, the brand has grown into a global success story, and all brand copy – web, social, press releases, packaging, Customer Service, and in-house operational copy – is still created following the original guidelines.

Chapter 38

A roadmap for creating a change program: the first six months

If you decide to create your brand voice with no outside help, here's a handy (and admittedly, comfortable) timeline for what you should be doing, when. It's based on worst-case timelines for big organisations.

Month 1: Audit for current status of the brand voice.

- Rate a selection of material from each of your channels, making sure you have copy created by both in-house writers and agency teams.
- Compare these to the brands you admire most or the brands which the leadership team talks about as an ideal.

Month 2: Listen for varying levels of dis/satisfaction with the brand voice.

- Conduct structured 1:1 interviews with key people to understand how they feel about the performance of the brand voice.

Month 3: Create the rationale for change.

- Calculate the cost – both human and commercial – of current underperformance against the ideal.
- Audit for where you can expect to achieve improvements.
- Create the Quick Wins Matrix and the Vocal/Influence Matrix.
- Calculate the costs of improvement against those matrices.
- Construct a timeline. Then double it.
- Book time in the calendar of the person who you'd like to be the project sponsor.

Month 4: Selling it in.

- Build a picture of how the brand stands against its competitors.
- Build a picture of how the brand stands against the most-admired brands.
- Be clear about the commercial impact of doing nothing and the upside of changing, while being honest about the robustness of the figures.
- Bring in the results of the selected listening project.
- Be honest about the roadblocks that you'll expect to face.
- Be clear about a reasonable (i.e., the doubled) timeline.
- Critically, build a sense of urgency. Be clear about what will happen if nothing changes. Avoid 'immediate catastrophe', but instead, focus on the problems that you reasonably expect in the next half-year, full year, and two years.
- Listen for objections. Handle. Live with the decision.

Months 5–6: Build the Change Team and get the Quick Wins.

- With a clear mandate (and budget) for change from the CEO, engage a senior guiding team with the influence and authority to make decisions and provide support. Use this team to prepare a shared vision for the change program. Make clear that they are not being asked to sign off recommendations but, instead, to be actively involved, with a considerable addition to their workload.

- Use the Quick Wins (Impact × Difficulty) Matrix to execute your Quick Wins. Communicate up, down, and left-to-right about these Quick Wins. The project sponsor needs to know. So, too, do the people who are most heavily impacted by the program. So do your guiding team – it's too easy to think that they have seen the changes and understood what a great success this is. You need their continued help.

LONG-LASTING CHANGE DEPENDS ON SOLID PREPARATORY WORK

Chapter 39

The roadmap: months 6–12 and 12–24

It's possible to accelerate these timelines. We have produced guidelines in eight weeks. Although once we'd done the 'difficult bit' of creating the guidelines, we still had to generate a lot of energy persuading people this was the right thing to do.

Here's a plan for the second six months of a 'comfortable' timing plan for a large organisation.

Months 6–8: Share the vision and the change program.

- Build a picture of how this will change daily life. Be clear and simple in what you are communicating.
- Start focussing on the harder to change issues.

Months 9–12: Remove barriers to progress: build SkAD.

- In our experience, the three things that limit performance in a team are Skills, Authority and Direction.

  Help the team by offering training and coaching specifically focussed on what they need to improve in their skills.

  Engage people in the change program by giving them more authority to make the changes required.

  Use the Vision you created previously to give them a clear direction of how the brand voice will develop and the direction that this will take the company – and their teams – in.

- Deal with the Resistors, patiently. Most people aren't coming in to work to actively undermine things. They have their reasons. Listen carefully (don't just re-explain why change is critical). Fix what you can, be honest about what you can't. Ask them to align with the program and give it their support – if they still feel unable to do that, then avoid confrontation, but be clear how you will seek to remove their resistance. Then quickly focus elsewhere – nothing sucks energy out of a system so much as a single malcontent that demands too much attention. Even if you can't change them, you can change everything around them, leaving them isolated ultimately.

And after that?

Months 12–24: Map your progress, keep going...

- After one year, get people to recommit by rerunning the analysis on the commercial and human rationale for change.
- Be honest about mistakes and anything that means the goals have changed.
- Be patient.
- Never stop communicating.

> YOU CAN ACCELERATE THIS
> TIMELINE. JUST MAKE SURE
> YOU DON'T MISS ANY STEPS

Case study #7

A much-loved British fashion brand that now
needed to compete internationally.

'Why do we even need any words at all?'

It's quite a challenge to be asked by a CMO to help their Creative Director with the brand language, only for the Creative Director to open the conversation with those words.

But any question that attacks first principles, those things we've just assumed must be true, is always worth thinking about.

The Creative Director, who had a beautiful visual aesthetic sense, was, in fact, voicing something that lies beneath a lot of the conversations among brand teams at luxury goods companies. Their world is dominated by visual imagery. Do they even need language?

At first glance, you don't. A beautiful product, beautifully shot, placed in just the right media, does a great job. Why do you need language?

Perhaps at the start of the customer journey, you might not. At that moment, you're trying to draw people's eyes to look at you. It's a long time before you're trying to make them consider you. The route to the mind is through the soul.

But our company has an expression: 'Visuals attract, verbals engage'. And it's still true in the luxury world. What you need are enough words to anchor your emotional message, a piece of rational Velcro that sticks to the customer's mind.

Maybe it's for their internal rationalisation. Perhaps it's so they can place their purchase in a story when they tell people about it. But language is always necessary.

And brand language becomes more important the further along the customer journey you go. As a customer moves from treating the product like eye candy to wondering whether it can be part of their life, the brand needs to make a very personal connection.

The customer will start asking questions – some overtly, some only in their mind. In this situation, using a distinctive brand language to conjure a story is critical. Having one voice is essential.

For this British fashion house, our first task was to map out along the customer journey each point where language would be needed and what it should do at that time.

As always, we dug deep into the brand's archaeology to understand its DNA. We conducted carefully constructed interviews throughout the organisation. We listened to customers, we listened to competitors.

When we'd defined the voice on all three levels, we mapped how it should work along the customer journey.

For each moment, we looked at both what written content there should be and how much of it: going from very little at the beginning, then increasing as the customer's relationship with the brand deepened.

We knew, for example, that in the luxury sector, there is generally very little language used in the above-the-line advertising. But in-store, there are brief descriptions of each product and conversations which can be guided with key phrases and a clear narrative. Post-purchase, there is far more language involved in Customer Service and CRM content.

After a period of consultation, we presented our language recommendations back to the brand team. The work was approved. But we knew we had really brought the brand team along with us when we overhead a very heated conversation about the use of just one word in a piece of copy.

We had further proof of the brand voice's uptake when the brand's Head of HR asked us to use the definition of the brand voice to help shape the Employee Values program that she was creating.

Chapter 40

Making sure your guidelines are used every day

Too often, expensive guidelines gather dust in a bottom drawer.

Good design can help your guidelines inspire writers every day.

A few years ago, we were contacted by the CEO of the UK clothing label Fred Perry. Perhaps 'clothing label' isn't the best description. The brand inspires intense loyalty amongst its fans of musicians, football fans, and designers. This loyalty is first inspired by the unchanging style of Fred Perry's iconic tennis shirt. But as you get to know the brand, you're drawn into a backstory of Fred Perry, the man – world tennis champion, businessman, and iconoclast. Apparently, Tom Ford won't play tennis in anything else.

The challenge for selling their iconically designed tennis shirt online was just that: the shirt is unwavering in its design. Some people find it indistinguishable from a polo shirt by Ralph Lauren selling for three times as much or a supermarket version at a tenth of the price.

To make Fred Perry's situation harder, the brand sells its iconic tennis shirts in two ranges: 'Authentic' is the entry-level range for the genuine, original tennis shirt and the more expensive range is under the 'Laurel Wreath' label.

The CEO told us that his writers were having difficulty differentiating their writing in the two ranges. This is a problem when you're asking people to pay 35% more for one shirt than another – and they're comparing the two shirts on a phone screen that's six cm across.

The CEO also told us that his company didn't have a large marketing team – certainly not enough to constantly police whether writers were adhering to the guidelines. However, there was throughout the company a great attention to design and a love of the tactile nature of things.

We asked whether we could design a subset of the verbal brand guidelines once the full set had been signed off. They would be printed on high-quality paper with foil printing. Instead of being a turgid, indexed book, it would be a hand-sized fold-out pamphlet. As you opened it out, it would take you deeper and deeper into the brand, revealing more about the target market and the brand's narrative, Tone of Voice, and key phrases.

Because we made the format of the guidelines represent the emotion of the brand as much as the factual content, and because we built them to be tactile, accessible, and practical, we found the guidelines were kept on top of the writers' desks and referred to on a daily basis.

The continual presence of the brand books meant that they

were easy to refer to. But they were also a constant reminder of the importance of the differentiated Fred Perry brand voice.

Not all brands have the love of design – or the designers – that Fred Perry has.

But almost everyone has a competitive streak, and there's a way you can use that to encourage your writers to use the guidelines often.

> **DESIGN YOUR VERBAL IDENTITY GUIDELINES TO BE USED EVERY DAY – AND THEY WILL BE**

Chapter 41

Creating living guidelines

Writers aren't lonely souls. In my experience, they're often proximal workers: not happy to be in the middle of the hubbub, not happy to be completely isolated, either. Instead, there's a happy equilibrium of sitting with headphones on, in the corner of the office or in a busy coffee shop.

How, then, can you keep them tuned in to the brand voice? A dry 140-slide PowerPoint document won't do that.

A 'Living Brand Voice Minisite' will.

Most brand guidelines are put online for people to refer to.

But there's a lot more you can do with the digital format.

We've found that the writers refer more often to the online guidelines if we add an interactive section where the writers from all the different agencies, working in different channels, in different time zones, can post the work they're proud of.

Then, you can give writers the power to upvote the work they like. (No downvoting allowed.) At the end of each month, the brand director or CXO can spend ten minutes sending an email to all their agencies, pointing out whose work was most upvoted.

We've discovered that, despite writers' love of sitting somewhere else with their headphones on, there's something very motivating for them in seeing other writers' output. And there's something even more motivating for seeing that work being highly praised.

There's also something motivating for the leaders of the bigger agencies when they see smaller agencies' work being praised more than their own.

There's one other thing we've found useful in encouraging writers to make regular use of the guidelines. It's to reward each month's winner – and to do it visibly.

So, as the writer sits there in the office, or in the giant pen in the centre of their agency (wishing they could have the solitude of a busy coffee shop), wondering why there's always a ratio of four designers (each with giant Mac Pro screens) to one writer (with a tiny ThinkPad), being given a visible reward in front of their colleagues for winning 'writing of the month' is a wonderful thing.

It can be cakes. It can be a shoulder massage while they work. Whatever it is, it's visible to the workers around them.

It's amazing what a little budget and some healthy competition will produce.

> **YOUR GUIDELINES ARE MORE INSPIRING WHEN THEY'RE CONSTANTLY UPDATED**

Chapter 42

You say tomato, I say tomato

Did a US senator really say, when asked whether they supported bilingualism in schools, 'If English was good enough for Jesus Christ, it should be good enough for us'?

As much as we like to think someone did say it (and it's been attributed to at least three different people), there's a more important point at work here: we all want our own language to be good enough for everyone else – but we know it can't be.

When brand teams ask if they'll need to adapt all of the verbal brand guidelines for every market which doesn't share their language, the answer is a simple No.

The advantage of having defined your brand voice on all three levels is that, for most of the time, you're not laying down rules for specific words. Instead, you're mapping out how your brand relates to the world, how it should come across in its tonal values, and how it's constructed on the page.

It's only in the section on 'Words and Phrases we do/don't use' in the Ground Level that you need to do something other than a straight translation.

And here, it's worth investing in a transcreation service rather than a translation agency. You want the nuance of individual phrases to be carried into other languages, so that they can become as much a part of your brand identity as a logo or a physical artefact.

(Of course, even transcreation isn't possible, which is why Mini's Spanish Twitter bio describes itself as 'la casa del go-kart feeling'.)

There are some things which are more difficult to negotiate. I remember a discussion, more than 25 years ago, with a French account handler at a London advertising agency. She explained that the brand's copy couldn't use the same rhythm and short sentences when it was to appear in French.

Her argument was that in French, short sentences aren't used. I was so surprised I didn't know what to say at first. Of course, the French use short sentences. What she meant was that the commonly accepted styling for brand copy doesn't use short sentences.

But the whole point of creating a differentiated brand voice is to create value by standing out. If anything, in this case, it seemed there was a greater opportunity to create value by keeping the copy's style intact when it was translated into French.

Again, if you've defined the higher levels of the voice, why the brand is speaking the way it is, then there shouldn't be much room for discussion at the Ground Level – 25 years ago, we didn't have the advantage of clear brand voice guidelines, and the discussion took up an hour with us in London and an equal amount of time in Paris.

There is one area where I think there needs to be an adaptation to different cultural values when you're adapting your style guides. And that's when you choose to use swearing or references to deities. What is acceptable in one country may be offensive, or even illegal, in another.

When you've got the guidelines adapted, and everyone's bought into the need for a new voice, there's the small matter of encouraging everyone to use them every day.

> **DEFINE YOUR BRAND VOICE ON ALL THREE LEVELS, AND YOU SAVE TIME AND MONEY ADAPTING THE VOICE IN DIFFERENT REGIONS**

Chapter 43

Training, explaining, and complaining

Here's the old model for learning: push them in a classroom, shout the information at them, test them, and shame them. Or was that just my school?

When I was being trained at work, it was different. We'd be invited into a classroom and have the information talked at us; we were then tested and sent back to our desks. We only found out the results of the assessment at the end of each year.

Not much has changed in the way most people run training, including how little I've learned in this way.

A new way of teaching is needed.

If all you want to do is give people information, don't invite them into a classroom; send them a PDF. Only invite someone into a classroom if you want to help them learn.

And only help someone to learn if you know which of their behaviours you want to change.

The first thing you want to ask before you start teaching someone is: what behaviours do I want to change? Or even better, what behaviours do I want our writers to do more of, which behaviours do I want them to maintain, and what do I want them to stop doing? This will make your training more focussed.

The next question you can ask yourself is: how can I understand why they do those things now, so I can help them change?

In the usual model of training, 80% of the time and the budget is spent on formal classroom-based sessions, into which everyone has been enrolled. At the end of this program, any remaining budget is spread thinly across all the attendees to give them some kind of follow-up.

In organisations which are most successful at changing behaviours and getting writers to adopt the voice quickly, training happens in a different way.

Only 20% of their time and budget is spent on formal classroom training. Before the project kicks off, there's a careful researching of who are the most likely candidates to benefit from the training. Who is most important to train now? Who's too busy to change behaviour at this time? Who's motivated to change right now? Will their changed behaviour have a significant impact on the wider organisation, or will they remain an island?

In the newer model, around 40% of the budget has been reserved for sessions after the formal classroom. In this phase, there's very specific coaching which is matched to individuals' or groups' needs. This is often 1:1 coaching, and it's where the biggest changes in behaviour start to happen.

The remaining budget is given to an ongoing program which creates sustainable change by embedding the learnings into daily life. This is done with regular communications (ideally, a trickle feed of digestible, ultra-practical tips) along with refresher classes and, most powerfully of all, 'coaching'.

> **CLASSROOM TRAINING ISN'T FOR SHARING INFORMATION; IT'S FOR CHANGING BEHAVIOUR**

Chapter 44

Coaching your writers

The temptation when you're helping writers (and nonwriters) improve their skills is to jump in and do it for them. Which you'll obviously resist.

And then there's the temptation to share your experience and give advice on how to fix a piece of writing. Which isn't a terrible thing to do when time is tight, and you need something fixed. You can even call it mentoring, if you're feeling generous.

But if your ultimate goal is to improve the skills of a particular person or team who are writing for you, nothing beats coaching for creating long-term improvements.

Coaching is much more time-consuming and mentally draining – and that's probably why it's so effective.

Our advice is to coach in 1:1 sessions or, even better, with one coach to two writers. That way, they get to see what's happening through another person's eyes, and they get the chance to become accountability partners to each other.

We believe that a writing coach almost always has to come from outside the organisation. Coaching feels personal, and it's hard for someone to open up to another person they see around the building. But there's something more than that.

Coaching is always a specialist skill, and being able to coach a writer depends on having an even rarer set of skills.

In the coaching sessions, your coach should be talking about more than just what's going on the page. One of the biggest determinants of the quality of the final output is how long you put off writing the first draft: so, an experienced, specialist writing coach can help with topics like procrastination and prioritisation plans.

Having a coach who's recognised as a good writer themselves is useful for several reasons. Mostly, it's about building trust. Only an experienced writer has tips which are useful and proven about how you can learn to write faster, as well as how you keep finding inspiration when the work is piling on, and how you can persuade yourself to critique your own work every time.

All the time, the coach wants to keep the primary responsibility for the writing with the writer, building their confidence as much as their skills.

There are certain things that a good coach will always do:

- Listen more than talk.
- Ask more than tell.
- Praise twice as much as criticise.

There are some other things a coach can do which are less obvious, such as limiting a writer's goals to just one or two points at a time over the course of the coaching program.

A structured program is important – and disproportionately valuable compared to one or two sessions. When both the coach and the writer know there is time ahead of them, the coach can reinforce the writer's confidence by pointing out practical signs of progress related to the goals.

The idea of having goals is a key part of the coaching program: what are you trying to get out of your writers? Faster? Better quality? More self-critiquing?

And how would you measure those practically?

When you have clear goals and a structured program, then you can also supplement your writers' improvements by nurturing communities of practice.

> **COACHING WRITERS IS A SPECIALIST SKILLSET**

Chapter 45

Smoking behind the bike sheds

When you're at school, you think that learning only happens when you're sitting in the classroom. Later, you realise you can learn outside on a pitch when you're being coached. Make the mistake of being caught smoking behind the bike sheds, and you'll be reminded that you learn a lot more from the people you choose to have around you.

People learn in a variety of ways. Street gangs, actuaries in seminars, salesmen meeting up for the regular Friday lunch – listen, and what you'll hear is them sharing tips and tricks and solving problems-in-common.

This is the idea behind 'communities of practice' – what goes on outside the classroom is at least as important for someone's learning and problem-solving as what goes on inside.

Writers are problem solvers – whether that's finding a new way to describe yet another 32" flat-screen TV or convincing people to switch their bank after 30 years. And problem solvers are better at solving problems when they can get together and share.

The idea of communities of practice emerged in the 1990s from anthropologist Jean Lave and theorist Étienne Wenger. They noticed that most ways of thinking about how learning happened assumed it's something which people do as individuals and is 'separated from the rest of our activities'.

Instead, when they realised how we all naturally acquire knowledge from our peers by sharing stories, they saw that formal learning in organisations was missing something important.

A community of practice can be a long name for something quite simple. At its core are three elements:

- a 'shared domain of interest' (writing)
- a committed community engaged in joint discussions to help each other (the writers)
- a 'shared repertoire of practice' such as experiences, stories, tools, and ways of addressing recurring problems

We've repeatedly found that sustaining a new, differentiated voice over time depends on creating communities of practice for your writers.

What works well is a 'last Friday of the month lunch'. It's important that everyone's in the room together – there's something different when you can see the smiles and share the same pizza. Dialling in on Hangouts or Zoom is fine for one or two people, but the bulk of the action has to be in the room.

Have a 'light' topic to kick things off. No need for an agenda or chairperson. A few subjects are thrown out, and there's a murmur of agreement around one. Don't bother with formal notetaking. Street gangs do well without minuting their meetings.

There can be the solving of new problems ('I'm stuck. Can we brainstorm?'). Offers of assets to be reused ('I've got a handy checklist I use before posting; anyone else want it?'). Or requests for simple information. All of these are problems which are slowing people down, and all being solved quickly and universally by a Friday lunchtime pizza. Sorry, I meant a community of practice.

A variety of experience is important. Lave and Wenger observed many different apprenticeships (midwives, tailors, US Navy quartermasters, people on the road to sobriety in AA) and saw in all of them how newbies initially join communities and learn at the periphery. As these people become more competent, they become more involved in the main processes of that community. Sessions end with a checkout from each person around the table. Some things are fixed, some things are picked up the next time. Some things are forgotten about. But in all of this, the rest learn from the best – and everyone is best at something.

> **WHEN YOU START A COMMUNITY OF PRACTICE FOR YOUR WRITERS, YOU'RE ACCELERATING LEARNING AND GOOD BEHAVIOURS IN YOUR ORGANISATION**

Chapter 46

Monitor, measure, improve

You're asking people to give up a lot of their time when you change the way they write. You're also spending a lot of money creating change. But the biggest thing you're contributing is your professional capital. So, you need to be able to show how things are working out for your company – and correct your course if necessary.

You can use both input goals and output goals to monitor how things are going, track them over time, and look for places where you can improve effectiveness.

The output goals are similar to the measures of most brand campaigns. The challenge here is that many of these measures will be influenced by more activities than just the brand writing.

For example, you're likely to be tracking brand awareness among your target groups as well as sentiment towards the brand. Some of this will be attributable to a changed brand voice, but it's hard to measure.

An area where brand language will have a much more obvious

impact is in the Awareness of Key Values (you can construct a simple AKV score). Once you have defined your audience and defined the key values your brand wants to be known for, you can track this quarter-on-quarter with a combination of quant and qual research. It's likely that people's awareness of your key values will be much more directly influenced by your brand writing than any other comms because it's those values you're writing to when you define your 10,000 ft narrative.

Another area strongly influenced by your writing will be your target market's awareness of your Thought Leadership. You can measure this by looking at the key topics where you want to be seen as Thought Leaders, then look at how often you're quoted or referenced. This is a simple measure to compare quarter-on-quarter to see how you're progressing.

The final output goal we like to measure is Engagement. Today, consumers want to be in a dialogue with brands they like. If your consumers aren't engaging with you, then your writing needs to work harder.

There are three simple input goals it's worth looking at as well.

The first of these reflects the growing need for businesses to be agile. Calculating the average time-to-publish (measure the time between briefing and publishing) shows how well your writing is keeping up with the needs of the business and the changes in the market. It's worth comparing departments on this measure, then trying to understand what makes some departments faster than others.

One client we worked with recently saw that the time-to-publish for their Investor Relations communications was taking almost five times as long as any other written communications. Was this because of poor writing skills? Was a higher standard required before approval? A poor process? A briefing malfunction? It started becoming easier to spot the issues, ask the questions, and make improvements only once they'd started measuring and comparing the different times-to-publish.

A similar measure is cost-to-publish (based on writer budgets). It's also valuable to compare this metric between departments and between in-house and agency creators.

The final value we ask to measure is writer satisfaction on a quarterly or twice-yearly schedule.

A happy writer is about 30% more productive than a 'satisfied' writer. An unhappy writer is worse than unproductive; they drag other people back.

Happy writers stay with you for longer, they grow in their skill-sets and contributions.

Writer happiness seems to be an uncanny early predictor of the future success of your brand voice and its impact on your business.

> **MEASURING YOUR NEW BRAND VOICE GIVES YOU THE OPPORTUNITY TO MAKE IT MORE EFFECTIVE**

Chapter 47

Run everyone through the sheep dip

How crazy would it be to allow only a handful of HR people to hear about an important HR policy? And you wouldn't want a new expenses policy to be followed only by someone in Finance. So why would you want only the marketing team to be aware of the new brand voice?

The brand voice isn't just how you speak to your customers and external shareholders. It's how everyone in your company conceptualises and expresses your brand to each other and to external stakeholders. And 'brand' is only a fancy name that people like me use to describe what other people call your reason to exist, your story, your margin.

Why wouldn't you encourage the whole company to use your new brand voice?

After all, everyone with a keyboard is writing for your company, adding or subtracting some small value each time they write. And everyone with a voice is doing the same.

When HR teams write their employee values, the style they choose (authoritarian, paternalistic, avuncular, whatever it is) becomes part of their message.

When your recruitment team writes about a job ad, if they express the opportunity in a way that shouts your brand values through your brand voice, you have a greater chance of hiring someone who's right for your brand.

When your retail team is trained in how they can use the brand voice, the team is more likely to use it when they speak to customers.

When your Head of Production uses your brand voice (especially referencing your 10,000 ft narrative) to speak to suppliers, the suppliers are more likely to believe in your brand and understand what's different compared to the other companies they supply. And maybe those suppliers can start to see themselves as partners and start to think about doing things differently with you.

The great Wally Olins said your brand is the central organising thought for your whole company. That's true, and your brand voice is the way that thought is conveyed from person to person throughout your company and beyond.

The most common way of getting everyone to use your brand voice is to arrange for the CEO to introduce it at an all-company meeting. They can talk about the importance of the brand and the role of the voice. Even better, they can throw out an offer of training sessions for anyone who wants to learn more about writing in the brand voice. That's anyone, not just writers.

This will champion good writing throughout the organisation, and it'll help you discover those people in the building who are keen writers but don't currently have 'writer' in their job title.

On the day I'm writing this, I've just come back from running a training course at a large UK retailer. One of the writers in the group had started as a store assistant. I'm not sure how the company found out she wanted to be a writer, but I already know she'll be great. She's enthusiastic, and she's spent every day of her early career working with the voice already.

Once you've introduced everyone to your company's voice, you just have to keep things going.

> **EVERYONE IN YOUR COMPANY CAN
> ADD VALUE WHEN THEY KNOW
> HOW TO USE YOUR BRAND VOICE**

Chapter 48

Keeping the flywheel turning

When you've successfully defined your brand voice, it feels like 'job done!' But it's really only Day 1.

And when you've got the training and coaching program going, you can feel like you're engaged in the biggest part of the work – but this is only 49% of the job of creating a long-term, highly differentiated voice for your company.

What's the remaining 51%?

Did you ever read the book *Good to Great* by the leadership legend Jim Collins? He said that some organisations stick at being good, while a few go on to be great. What was the difference?

In his description, he says the movement from good to great is not done in one giant leap. Instead, he compares it to the effort required to get a giant, heavy flywheel turning. You need relentless effort to build the momentum, even when it feels like nothing is really happening. But there comes a point when you achieve momentum. And then you have to keep going.

What keeps the flywheel turning when you're sustaining long-term change in your brand voice? It can be a few simple things.

Regular refresher emails. Before you run any training course, write eight to twelve short emails. Each one should be just two or three sentences focussed on a specific aspect of the voice. Send out one email each week after the training, as a gentle nudge to your writers.

Nourish the internal comms network. I've never found a Head of Internal Comms who didn't want more content. Especially well-written content. As 'everyone with a keyboard is a writer', use internal comms to broadcast what the new brand voice is and why it's valuable to everyone in your company.

Lunch and learn. Get your writers together once a month or once a quarter to listen to someone from outside your organisation talk about how they approach writing.

Scorecarding. Every six months, reaudit your copy. You don't have to review everything. A dozen pieces from each channel is fine and takes only a couple of hours. It's only when we measure things that we change them.

Clinics. Run drop-in sessions that are open to anyone, not just writers. If you have a Head of Copy, they can run this. If you don't have a Head of Copy, an external writer offers more than advice: they bring fresh eyes and no hierarchy, making it feel like a safe space to discuss problems.

Red Button Support. Sometimes, you have lots of firepower in your writing department, but not enough time. Or you have the firepower and the time but not enough distance to spot what's not right with a piece of work. If you find a great external writer that you trust – and who your external agencies trust – ask them to be on call. In this role, they're a quiet counsel to help you avoid that demotivating moment when you have to say, 'It's not right, but I just can't say why. Have another go.'

In the ideal situation, you'd be able to do everything you need. But what if your situation is less than ideal?

> ## THE DIFFERENCE BETWEEN A GOOD BRAND VOICE AND A GREAT ONE IS THE EFFORT YOU PUT IN AFTER 'EVERYTHING'S DONE'

Chapter 49

What if you can't
do everything?

Few people have all the budget and all the time they want. What
do you do then?

If you only have a day: Lock yourself in a room. Spend the
morning picking four or five areas of your communications
(perhaps samples from your advertising, website, social media,
Customer Service, and a report by the CEO).

Spend a couple of hours in the afternoon doing the same for
the leader in your sector. Then prepare a presentation showing
the inconsistencies in your voice and comparing it with how
consistent your competitors' language is.

Spend the early evening drawing up a commercial rationale for
updating your brand voice, showing where costs are currently
incurred and what might happen if you improve the voice.

Before you present it to your leadership team, find an hour to compile the Quick Wins Matrix so you've got a call to action for the team to latch on to.

If you have a week: Be comprehensive in your analysis of your own brand voice and that of your main competitors. Also, take a look at fast-growing Challengers in your sector. Don't forget to look at 'best-in-world' brands from other sectors.

Then compile a Board-ready audit of the brand voice, showing what your underperforming voice is costing you and what it would take to change.

If you have a fortnight: As well as a Board-ready audit, run the 5 Whys exercise to get to the bottom of some of the causes of why your brand voice isn't right. Prepare an estimate of the ROI for fixing things. Remember to mix hard values with human values (e.g., our team is working three weekends out of four, which is fine, but 80% of that time, the work is then thrown out).

If you have a month: Do the Board-ready brand voice audit and the examination of the causes and skillsets issue. But also, hire a freelance writer who is highly flexible in their style (not just highly rated by the last place they worked) and pay them 20% more than anyone else in your department. Make sure they are also highly empathetic and able to explain their thinking. Before they start, pick your priority communications, so you don't spread them too thinly.

Look for the impact their writing has had externally on engagement levels and look for the impact it's had internally on inspiring writers.

Try to put a financial value on that impact and then use it to support your case for a program that updates your brand voice.

If you have eight weeks: Build A/B test programs, focussing on just one product or channel.

Build your case to show how effective a changed voice has been in those areas, along with the commercial impact. Support this with anecdotal evidence from your customers and your team to show how much better their life has become with the new voice.

> **YOU CAN CREATE SOME CHANGE IN JUST A WEEK OR A COUPLE OF MONTHS**

Chapter 50

One final thought on change

Everyone knows that change isn't easy. What's rarely talked about is that when you lead a change process, you yourself have to change.

You will have to step out of your comfort zone.

You will have to put your own job on the line definitively and actively, rather than in any blurred way.

Unless you have superb influencing skills, you'll need to acquire them quickly.

And developing patience will be important.

There'll be a lot of hunch work. But you'll also need to show how you've moved from hunch to recommendation.

What's always underestimated in proposing a change program is the amount of change required by the person leading the program.

> YOU WILL CHANGE AS YOU CHANGE THE COMPANY AROUND YOU.
> BUT WASN'T THAT THE OBJECTIVE ALL ALONG?

SECTION 4

USEFUL RESOURCES FOR WRITERS AND THEIR MANAGERS

Chapter 51

Modern grammar is a class war

'Some method should be thought on for...fixing our language for ever.'

JONATHAN SWIFT, 1712.

Language changes. Grammar evolves. Complaints about it, however, appear to be constant.

I was taught my grammar at school 40 years ago. I was taught it by someone who'd learnt their grammar 30 years before that. Should I still be bound by the same conventions? Should I be writing like someone speaking from before World War II? If society moves on, shouldn't language?

There are two kinds of rules in the world: those which exist to codify something to keep it regular and the kind of rules which exist to make sure everyone plays fair. Sometimes I think that when people criticise others for not following the rules of grammar, they're actually upset that someone seems to be cutting corners and cheating.

Any rule of grammar exists only to help make our meaning clear. I don't believe it should be the other way around: we shouldn't change how we speak just to follow rules if doing so would restrict our ability to make our content and our attitude better understood.

Now, I can choose to ignore a rule of grammar if I believe that following the rule would make what I'm saying less clear. For a company, it's more complicated.

What could be more soul-sapping to a CMO than to have to stop all the other parts of the efforts to grow the company, just to have a conversation about whether there should, or shouldn't, be a comma in a sentence?

This is why it's critical to have all the levels of your brand voice clear at the beginning. Your language conveys more than just its content. The language style you use also signals what you stand for and the kind of world you believe in. Conservative or progressive? Rule-bound or adventurous? Considerate or gung ho? It's those choices which should dictate how you codify your grammar.

However, no grammar book I've ever read has addressed the real issue that is swirling in the dark waters beneath the surface of these arguments. Grammar is a class war: the ignorant greengrocer is laughed at by the educated middle classes for not knowing that he's misplaced his apostrophe. But if we do that, shouldn't we also be laughing at the middle-class professional who peppers their report with exclamation marks to emphasise the presence of their weak jokes? When you swim in these dark waters, you can catch your foot on a shopping trolley and get into trouble!!!!!

The most important thing is to build agreement with your team on your grammar styling. Take a look at the next chapter to find the things to agree on.

Once you've agreed on them (hopefully with decisions which reinforce your brand voice's narrative), then there's one more thing to do: quickly laminate your company's grammar style guide and get on with the real work.

Just make sure you cover all of the things that are likely to come up.

> **GRAMMAR'S RULES AREN'T 'RULES'.**
> **DECIDE WHAT YOU BELIEVE IN**
> **AND MOVE ON**

Chapter 52

Where to stick your apostrophes

There are some points of grammar which it's easy to agree on quickly. There are some things which (despite what other people claim) are open for discussion. And there are some things up with which, we will not put.

Let's start with things which are so widely agreed that diverging from them would seem careless:

- Apostrophes to show possession (e.g., the apple's weight)
- Capitalizing the first letter of names and places and the word which starts a sentence
- You're and your, their and there and they're

Things which are disputed, but you need to agree on, for your style guide:

- Lists, commas, and the Oxford comma
- Are collective nouns to be treated as singular or plural? E.g., 'The BBC have changed their logo' or 'The BBC has changed

its logo'. (Technically, the second version is correct, except that as we no longer want to portray organisations as mono-lithic bodies, I recommend the first version.)
- Modern sentences. Do they need verbs and nouns? Can they be broken in two? Or more?
- Whether we use contractions such as you're, he'll, we'll, or write them out in full
- Whether we care if there's a difference between 'shall' and 'will'. Same for 'might' and 'may'
- How you signal the start of quoted speech, 'If you know what I mean'
- Whether you capitalise the names of Seasons, Personified Nouns, Cardinal Points, words in titles, job titles

Then there are things which will irritate your team, and you'd do well to straighten out now:

- The preference for using the active voice and not the passive voice (Marvin Gaye never had a hit single 'It was heard by me through the grapevine'.)
- When you write numbers in numerals or words
- A preference for definite, concrete language
- When you use the semicolon (other than to signal that you had a university education)
- Making sure you link the verb in the sentence to its 'actor' (e.g., 'On leaving the country, his wife was much happier with him'. Who left? Him or his wife?)
- Whether you can start a sentence with conjunctions such as And, But, So, Or
- If you can split infinitives. I think you can, but traditionalists seem to vehemently disagree.
- Whether you can end a sentence with a preposition (like at, for, in, on, over, under, off)

- 'Which' vs. 'That'
- When to use adverbs or adjectives

In *Gulliver's Travels*, written by Jonathan Swift, Gulliver is confronted by a war between the Big-Endians and the Little-Endians. They were at war because they couldn't agree on which end of the boiled egg you should crack open. It was a satire on religion. But there are equally dogmatic battles about grammar.

And on this last note, I'd like to strike out and take a position. It's unnecessary to differentiate between It's and Its with an apostrophe. I can't think of a sentence whose meaning could be confused by omitting it. I'm sure there are some, but other languages manage fine without the possessive apostrophe. Its time we producers of language came together and made a stand.

> **THE IMPORTANT THING IS TO REACH AGREEMENT ON YOUR GRAMMAR CHOICES AND GET ON WITH THE REAL WORK**

Chapter 53

You can do better than readability scores

Managers are often challenged to make the qualitative things in life as measurable as the naturally quantitative. When we accept the challenge, we are in danger of losing some of the subtle value of qualitative work just to make it more instantly buyable by numerically biased people.

Which, sometimes, is a good enough reason to do it.

There are several formulae for measuring the readability of a piece of copy. The most popular is the Flesch–Kincaid score. This rates text against an average of US school grade levels. For example, a score of 8.0 means that a typical eighth grader would understand the document. The Gunning fog index sounds like a weather report for a Devon moor, but it shows how many years of formal education a person needs in order to understand the text on the first reading. The medical profession prefers the SMOG Formula: a Simple Measure of Gobbledygook.

But all the measures use simplistic formulae. The Gunning fog counts how many 'complex' words of more than three syllables there are. Yet some of those words can be easily understood, like 'television' or 'syllables'.

At their best, these formulae open up a conversation about readability. At their worst, they lead a writer into conjuring text which is hard to understand but scores well.

A greater danger is that people focus on the score's number, not its value. How much better is a 99 than a 77? Is the difference in 'quality' so big that it's worth rewriting the copy? Even if a 99 is better, does it have any impact on the business?

The Flesch–Kincaid will give you a very quick comparison. It'll show you that the Guardian newspaper is a lot harder to read than The Sun. But it doesn't tell you whether that's because of the subject matter, the worldview, or the language used. And it doesn't tell you why the publishers of The Sun are making more money than the publishers of the Guardian.

At Verbal Identity, we saw the need to develop a better method for scoring qualitative writing, and so we developed the Category Competition Index (CCI). This helps you see how successfully your brand language performs two essential tasks: proving your brand's membership of a sector by using the appropriate sector language and, secondly, using language to remain differentiated from your competitors.

The CCI includes the Flesch–Kincaid score as one metric because however distinctive your language is, you still want it to be readable. We also measure average sentence length. Shorter sentences win.

We look for copy that uses unnecessarily long words and copy which strays away from everyday English.

Here's a worked example for three British newspapers, a marketing trade journal, and the pilot's manual for flying the F16.

Category Competition Index

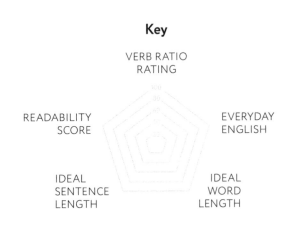

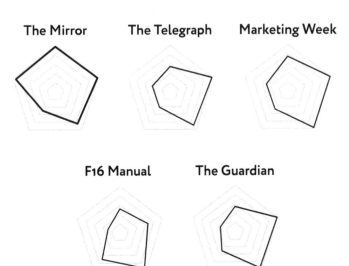

As you'd hope, the newspapers use everyday English, and the F16 doesn't. The Telegraph's readability score is a lot lower than The Mirror's. Does this mean The Telegraph isn't as well-written as The Mirror? No, it means that reading The Mirror requires fewer years of schooling.

The Verb Ratio Rating looks for that confusing 'management consultant' habit of making a noun out of a verb, e.g., 'We have a solve for this issue'. In the graph above, The Mirror excels at rooting out this problem. The Guardian has a fail for it.

The graph shows how the languages of The Telegraph and The Mirror differ. This in itself doesn't tell you which is better. But a reading of the graph reveals how the two papers are successfully signalling to their own readers what kind of person enjoys their paper.

As the CMO of a brand, you can use the CCI to see how similar or different you are from other brands in your sector and work out what aspect of their language you can ask your writers to focus on.

> **READABILITY SCORES ON THEIR OWN PROVE NOTHING.**
> **IT'S THE INTERPRETATION WHICH GIVES INSIGHTS**

Chapter 54

Critiquing writers without tears (yours, not theirs)

Remember the acronym KISS: Keep It Simple, Stupid? There's a similar acronym for successfully managing writers:

KISAS – Keep It Short and Straight.

All writers like flattery. They're people, after all. But what they really want to know is exactly how to improve their work.

Keeping your feedback simple depends on picking just one or two things that you're asking them to improve. Even if you think the piece is riddled with bad writing, don't give more than three specific pieces of feedback.

If you give them more than that, the first problem is that they won't retain all of it. But the bigger danger is that you're slipping into giving dictation – move this from here to there, try to find something different to say here, don't use that word...

As soon as you're into giving dictation, you're cutting out the value of having a skilled writer, and you're only two meetings away from having to write it yourself.

So, if it seems to you like there's something you want to say on every page, what do you do?

Use the three levels of the voice to pinpoint what's not working.

Are all your comments about the tonal values of the writing? Or are they revealing a lack of appreciation of the brand voice's narrative? Is it the Ground Level Details which are wrong?

And to keep your feedback straight as well as simple, spend a moment to work out which stage of the writing process you think they need to improve: Understanding – Creating – Shaping?

First, does your writer really understand your product or service?

If they do, and the writing seems flat, it's likely a problem with the Creation process. Could you do anything to improve your briefing? Would they benefit from you inspiring them, for example, by showing other brands' copy which exemplifies what you're trying to achieve?

After any Creation phase, any good writer should go back and shape their work. Can you persuade them to allow some time on each project to self-critique: looking at the obvious things, but then also reviewing whether the piece matches the three levels of the voice?

At one time, we were acting as Red Button Support for a brand team and their ad agency: after the initial guidelines and training had been created, they were producing work in all their channels much faster. But there were occasional moments when a piece of copy wasn't quite right, and they needed to unpick what wasn't working.

On one occasion, the agency Creative Director called us up as a piece of her team's work had been thrown out. It was an ad due to appear in a national newspaper in a few days' time, with a significant media spend behind it. It had been rejected because 'it wasn't funny'.

I read the copy. It made me laugh.

But I realised the joke wasn't right for the brand. I spent some time with the writer looking back at the brand guidelines, how the brand's humour was defined, and exactly what kind of 'funny' they were. Once the writer – and client team – realised this, it was easy to rewrite, and they tried another style of humour to give the copy the lift it needed.

The client team approved it that day, and the ad went to press.

Once you've given feedback on the writing, is it time to worry about adding some style to the copy?

> **FOCUSSING ON THE THREE LEVELS OF YOUR BRAND VOICE IS THE BEST WAY TO GIVE FEEDBACK TO YOUR WRITERS**

Chapter 55

A note on style: don't

There are probably as many books written on good writing style as there are books on how to perfect your grammar. Both ideas are fallacious. There are no empirically provable rules of grammar. In commercial writing, an obvious style stands between the reader and the meaning.

Perfect clarity of message beats an obvious writing style every time. So, what advice for clarity?

George Orwell has six famous tips for achieving clarity in 'Politics and the English Language'.[2]

- Never use a metaphor, simile, or other figure of speech which you are used to seeing in print.
- Never use a long word where a short one will do.

---

[2] George Orwell, 'Politics and the English Language' (London, Great Britain, 1946), http://www.public-library.uk/ebooks/72/30.pdf.

- If it is possible to cut a word out, always cut it out.
- Never use the passive where you can use the active.
- Never use a foreign phrase, a scientific word, or a jargon word if you can think of an everyday English equivalent.
- Break any of these rules sooner than say anything outright barbarous.

In the same essay, he gave some less frequently shared tips:

Avoid a dying metaphor. As he explains, 'a newly invented metaphor assists thought by evoking a visual image, while on the other hand, a metaphor which is technically 'dead' (e.g., iron resolution) has in effect reverted to being an ordinary word'.

I remember the first time I heard the expression 'let's run it up the flagpole and see who salutes it'. I had a strong mental image of a parade ground, a flagpole, and a small number of soldiers. Now when I hear that expression, I assume someone is only using it ironically.

Avoid operators of verbal false limbs. He warns, 'instead of being a single word, such as *break, stop, spoil, mend, kill*, a verb becomes a *phrase*, made up of a noun or adjective tacked on to some general-purpose verb'. His examples include 'give grounds for', 'give rise to', and 'serve the purpose of'. 'Explain', cause', and 'is' might be good substitutes. So, avoid trying to switch it up.

Pretentious diction. Orwell's advice? 'Words like *phenomenon, element, individual* (as a noun), *objective, categorical, effective, virtual, basic, primary, promote, constitute, exhibit, exploit, utilize, eliminate, liquidate* are used to dress up a simple statement and give an air of scientific impartiality to biased judgments.'

All good advice. What else can you do?

Build a scrapbook of copy you like. Very handy for 9 p.m. on a Thursday night.

Build a folder of copy you don't like. Annotate it to remind you of what to avoid.

Good writing is good editing. Leave your writing in a drawer for as long as you can. 'Write drunk, edit sober' is good advice, but not to be taken literally.

Avoid the curse of knowledge. Always be aware of how much more you know than your reader. If in doubt, remember the frustration you felt the last time someone from IT told you how to fix your computer.

See your reader. Spend 30 seconds really imagining them. Where are they? What were they doing before? What interruptions are they likely to face while reading? What concerns them most?

Pick just one reader. For however many people you are writing to, you are only ever writing to one person. You cannot move a whole crowd with oratory, you can only move each person. Don't broadcast from one to many. Write from one, to one.

Finally, the single best piece of advice for any writer:

Read it out loud. Whatever slips you've made, you'll hear them. If your sentences are so long that you can't say them in one breath, your breathlessness will direct you. Repetitions and clumsiness, missteps, and loose logic, they all come to life when you read your writing out loud.

There are also some quick tips every writer and their manager could have pinned up somewhere in the office.

STRIVE FOR CLARITY OVER STYLE

Chapter 56

7 quick tips for quick writers

1. STRUCTURE CONTENT FOR THE READER'S BENEFIT, NOT YOURS.

There's something you can do to be more persuasive.

Most people start off by saying how important this new initiative is for the company. Then they give a few reasons why it's important. Then they say what they want the reader to do. Finally, they throw in what's in it for the reader.

That's the wrong way round.

Start by telling someone what's in it for them. Support that with well-reasoned argument. Finally, tell them why it's important to the company.

That will help you win your reader's attention and, eventually, their actions.

2. SURF, SWIM, DIVE. OR SINK.

Pay attention to the headlines and subject headers in your document.

Rarely will anyone read your complex document in one go or from front to back, absorbing all the facts. They jump around, skidding across one passage, then diving into something that is more appealing to them.

So, write headlines that grab their attention. Use subject headings that spike their interest. Create passages that make them want to immerse themselves.

3. PEOPLE REMEMBER NARRATIVES BETTER THAN FACTS.

I read an interesting paper in *Scientific American Mind*[3] magazine.

One group of students was asked to read Anton Chekhov's story 'The Lady with the Dog', about a well-to-do lady who had an affair. A second group read the story's key facts in the form of transcripts from divorce court proceedings. The two groups were tested a day later. The first group of students recalled far more facts than the second.

Narrative works. The end.

---

3   Oatley, Keith. 'In the Minds of Others'. *Scientific American Mind* 22, no. 5 (2011): 62-67. http://www.jstor.org/stable/24943457.

4. 'DO YOU THINK YOU CAN PASS THE SALT?'

Language helps us navigate social powerplay: of course, I can pass the salt, but the fact that you acknowledged that I don't have to pass the salt is understood and appreciated. Here's the salt.

You want the salt? Show them you understand that they don't have to pass it to you.

5. CHILD? ADULT? PARENT?

The 1970s Transactional Model of communication highlighted that at any time, we operate in one of three distinct modes – and so do our readers. Adult to Adult works. Parent to Child works. Speaking like a Parent to an Adult doesn't.

If you can work out the mode your reader is in, you can work out the best mode you should write in. Do they want advice? To be told what to do? To be asked for their esteemed input?

6. A ROSE BY ANY OTHER NAME

Every word or phrase comes with a long train of associated meaning. To check your writing, ask someone else to read it. Even better, ask a trained linguist how people will hear the words you say.

7. TALK TO A WRITER

If your subject is complex, or if it could influence revenue, or if it's trying to get other people to change their behaviour, ask a writer for advice.

Good writers are creative people, and there is nothing a creative person likes more than believing that there is someone else who thinks they have something worth listening to.

> **KEEP YOUR READER IN MIND, AND YOUR WRITING WILL ALWAYS BE BETTER**

Chapter 57

The robots are coming

(The danger with writing anything about computer-generated language is that it becomes out of date between typing the final full stop and hitting 'Publish'. So, here are some possibly out-dated thoughts.)

Simple 'language-from-numbers' processing has been used for decades. Weather reports can be created by software which takes numerical meteorological data as input and outputs short sentences that look as good as a human would have written.

Recently, Springer in Germany published a book written entirely by AI. And in 2020, an entire article was written for the Guardian newspaper in Britain by the GPT-3 software engine.

Well, almost. And not quite.

When you read the publicity announcement for the Springer book – which was written by a human – you wonder if that's where the software should've started. It's formulaic, it's confusing, and the sentences are full of nouns jumbled on top of each other like frogs in spring. Do we need to worry if machines are replacing this quality of writing?

The 1,100-word article in the Guardian ('A robot wrote this entire article. Are you scared yet, human?') was more startling.

It had a flow of ideas, clear paragraphing, and some attitude. Most impressive, it was in the style of the Guardian – thoughtful, mildly outraged, agitating. Overall, it was as good as almost anything else in the paper that day.

Except that the editors at the Guardian felt it necessary to write a note clarifying their process.

They'd had to kickstart the machine with a 50-word introduction, mapping out the territory it would cover. When the software produced eight different versions of an article, the editors had to cut them together to make something out of the best parts of each.

The editors say it took less time to edit than an op-ed created by humans. But you'd rarely give a writer a 50-word intro. And perhaps not map out the whole topic for them.

Natural language generation in business falls somewhere in the middle of all this.

Much of e-com writing by humans has become formulaic: a list of key facts around features or basic ingredients. As one writer at a major UK retailer told me, 'I'm an English Literature graduate, and I'm basically shelf-stacking words.'

As Amazon's domination of retail grows, we're being educated to expect less humanity from all parts of the retail experience, including reading about what we're buying. The English Literature graduates writing for the UK retailer have seen a 10× increase in the number of products they have to write copy for every day. There's no time for insight, empathy, and the other things which a skilled writer can put into copy to help build the confidence of the reader in the purchase. Those things aren't there, but we're no longer looking for them, either.

There are AI software companies that will create more impactful subject lines for email, more carefully crafted body copy, and a few other things.

This *does* mean that the end is in sight for jobs where a human is asked to maximise output and not worry about quality – that's a classic role for a machine. And as software is taught the nuances of a brand's language, a large number of writers' roles (in Customer Service, product information, social media content) will also disappear.

But there will still be a satisfying role for writers to use insight, empathy, and creativity to create charisma and loyalty.

Which is the most valuable part of marketing.

For years, the standard test of whether machine-generated language was 'good enough' was the Turing test: could it fool a human.

But maybe the ultimate standard will be the 'Marx Test' – named after Groucho, not Karl.

It'll be time for all writers to find something else to do when a machine can write a line as funny and nuanced as Groucho's disposition on time and daily life:

'Time flies like an arrow. Fruit flies like a banana.'

> **THE MACHINES AREN'T QUITE
> READY TO REPLACE THE WRITERS**

Conclusion
What I realised from writing this book

Finally, if you'll excuse me, I'd like to take a digression. It's into something that had been bothering me for ten years, ever since I started Verbal Identity, and which I only managed to resolve when I finished writing this book.

The issue is this: when I say you are a language animal, do I mean that you only use language to put a label on things? Or do I mean that since you happen to have language available in your head as a tool to construct things, can you use that language to conjure up completely new thoughts?

I've realised now that in the commercial world, this distinction matters.

When you hire someone to do some writing, are you asking them to describe more clearly what exists, or are you asking them to help your customers create something new?

The philosopher Charles Taylor, in his book *The Language*

Animal, draws a line between these two schools of thought of how language works. The early philosophers of language, such as Locke, Hobbes, and Condillac, believed that language could only serve an empirical function. There are a handful of ways of thinking about this. First, the function of language is to describe a thing which already existed before we started to describe it. Second, language can only describe 'metaphysically limited' things – things which are practically detectable. This makes language, to my ear, merely a tool for science-like behaviours.

But Professor Taylor says that if you and I believe language to have only a limited functionality, it means language cannot have a mind-expanding role when you and I are talking about aesthetic matters, or religious, political, and literary ideas. (This theory is supported by other language philosophers, including Hamann, Herder, and Humboldt, with the Batman and Robin of linguistic philosophy, Heidegger and Wittgenstein, piling in more recently.)

We know language describes things well. If I invite you to sit on a chair, I don't expect you to eat a grape.

But does language also help create new mental concepts? Could the use of romantic language lead me to experience love? Could you ask a writer to use language to help conjure an entirely new phenomenon, such as an emotionally significant mobile phone?

Linguistics matters more than dinner party conversation here. It matters because you need to know whether you are asking your writers to neatly describe what's in front of them or whether you're asking them to use language to give birth to new ideas.

Are you asking them to reflect or create?

The former is a large part of the commercial writing world, with mass globalisation leading to writers frantically banging away on laptops in Costa Rican coworking spaces, charging a penny a word to support their tropical habit.

But expecting a writer to create, to use language to bring into life something which might not have completely existed before, this is something special. It's a large part of the fiction-writing world, where great authors are paid for the effect their language creates. And it has a role in the commercial world, where we're asked to Think Different or Just Do It or understand how an iPad's battery capacity isn't measured in mAh, but in what it means we can now do in our lives. And it's the reason why a writer who charges more than a penny a word could radically change your business for you.

Perhaps that idea of language alone conjuring something new into being just sounds too far-fetched – until one day in your life, your heart leaps as a person in funny clothes, standing at the front of a special building, brings your new marital status into existence merely by saying the words 'I now pronounce you married.'

About the Author

CHRIS WEST is the Founding Partner of Verbal Identity, the world's most successful strategy agency specialising in the power of language. His firm has guided global and national brands, relaunches, and startups, from B2B and B2C to tech and luxury and everything in between, including LVMH, BASF, the John Lewis Partnership, TOMS, and the global skincare growth brand Votary.

A multi-award-winning copywriter, Chris also contributes to national newspapers and guest lectures at business schools. Chris lives in Oxford, England, with his wife, twins, and a handful of Siberian Forest cats.

You can find him online at verbalidentity.com.

9 781544 523569